ON THE WAY TO
BETHLEHEM

ON THE WAY TO
BETHLEHEM

*Reflections on Christmas
for Every Day in Advent*

by
Hilary McDowell

UPPER
ROOM BOOKS™
NASHVILLE

Cover Design: Kirk DouPonce, David Uttley Design, Sisters, Oregon
Cover Image: Tony Stone International
First printing in the USA: 2000

The Library of Congress Cataloging-in-Publication Data
McDowell, Hilary.
    On the way to Bethlehem : reflections on Christmas for every day in Advent /
by Hilary McDowell.
        p. cm.
    ISBN 0-8358-0920-X
    1. Advent—Meditations. 2. Christmas—Meditations. I. Title.
BV40.M29 2000
242'.33—dc21

00-027530

Printed in the United States of America

IN MEMORY OF MY AUNT ELLIE,
a faithful prayer giant,
whose consistent intercessions
on my behalf through the years
have been one of the mainstays
of my life.

CONTENTS

INTRODUCTION

✳

When God created the heavens and the earth, the first biblically recorded creative act upon the earth was the production and establishment of light. God generates it as an extension of himself who is the light. The Advent journey is a journey toward the light.

Intellectually and theologically such facts can be grasped and appreciated by way of the conduit of faith. The heart also cries out for enlightenment in the darkness of a sometimes lethargic and cynical world. There is another avenue toward understanding, less employed perhaps because of the potential danger inherent in its usage, the fact that it can sometimes be vulnerable to abuse or license. I refer to the imagination. But, disciplined by the precepts of scripture and guarded by the desire to share the truth of the incarnation of our Lord, a Christian imagination can sometimes be harnessed and employed to communicate experiential truth to both heart and head.

Weeks 1 and 2 of this book are a preparation to embark upon a journey of both intellect and heart, an experience of truth by way of sense as well as thought and understanding. It is "time travel" of the soul, engaging both thought and emotions. Annually, through the designated paths of traditional Christian worship, we visit Bethlehem. Sometimes, on vacation, our feet may literally tread the paths of the Holy Land. But, without leaving home, how often do we permit our heart to journey there and in openness and willingness to explore the familiar in a fresh manner, expecting God's touch upon our souls?

In the search for Jesus many books address the intellectual, many the theological aspects of our understanding. While not ignoring the importance of these aspects of the journey, I hope, nevertheless, to direct the journey toward the heart's cry for experiential truth. We need to know the pilgrim thirst of a present-day traveler working her way through a modern wilderness of the spirit with its many possible ambushes for the gift of wonder.

Because God has chosen, throughout my life thus far, to alternate his passage of entry to my soul between the twin portals of mind and heart, then I would be remiss not to share with you an open channel to the soul. From week 3 we move onward in the company of "the traveler."

The traveler in the book is not myself, but a combination, I hope, of the experiences of the many individuals who might walk this path through the passage of such a book. As you lift it to read, I invite you to say what I have learned to say to Jesus each year as I attempt the spiritual journey to Bethlehem and to Calvary, and onward: "Jesus, take me where you want me to go and let me never journey without you." King David left God & so sinned.

For the journey, imagine yourself in time travel, willing to let God surprise you with his presence, setting yourself within the shoes of "the traveler," thinking your way forward within the context of your own particular surroundings and circumstances. Redesign the decor to suit your situation while, at the same time, letting God touch your thoughts and heart in accordance with his wishes.

Try not to map the itinerary in your head. Keep within the events of scripture. Let God be the author of the story. The framework for each day's meditation might be:

* your own prayers of each day's present concern before reading;
* then the reading of the notes for the day, pausing for thought and prayer within this time as God prompts and inspires;
* the suggested prayer, perhaps used at the conclusion of your time of meditation, adding your personal comments to God of how you feel and how God has been speaking to you on that day.

On the Way to Bethlehem attempts to offer a vehicle to encourage you to etch your own progress in head and heart, as spiritually you journey toward Christmas this year. It traces a new passageway through the season and beyond. At journey's end it may resemble your own travel path only sketchily, but if we all, as pilgrims or seekers, travel in genuine search mode and with an eagerness to let God's presence permeate each day's time of silence, who knows where God will take us!

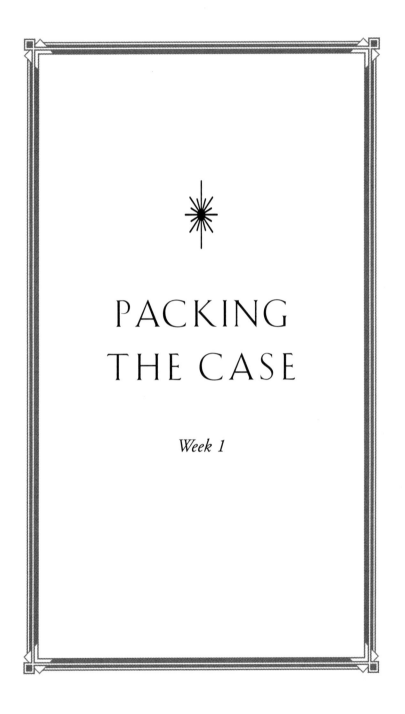

PACKING
THE CASE

Week 1

Week 1: ~~Sunday~~ Tuesday, *Nov 18, 03*
THE DECISION TO JOURNEY
Genesis 1:1–3 - *John 1:1-5*

Let there be light.

A choice lay ahead. The traveler could allow herself to be dragged toward Bethlehem this year, kicking and screaming through the tinsel-laden pressures of the expected route to Christmas. Already her local radio station had been announcing the countdown of the days even before the leaves had started to fall. Was the world getting more crazy, or was it just her?

Would she journey or not? All around her, folk were expressing the desire to stay at home, lock all doors, take the phone off the hook and opt out of the pandemonium. After all, hadn't she "been there, bought the T-shirt," year after year?

On the other hand, suppose she hadn't seen it all? Supposing God could surprise her? What if there was something at the destination more than shopping aisles and carols and mince pies?

She was already fed up with the shortening dark old days before Christmas, with their impending sanity-free workload of preparation, the anticipation of reaching the new year with a deep desire to lie in a darkened room until Spring. There was altogether too much darkness, in more ways than one.

Yes, she would go. Right from Genesis God had promised light and she owed it to herself to make the journey. What she dreaded was packing the case.

Drag the luggage from below the bed and set it out for a good airing. Slightly musty from months of disuse. Will it be big enough to hold all the necessities? Let's see—she selected the favorite clothes, the ones which made her feel and look the best. Then in went the protection from the sun, protection from cold, and lots of underwear.

Better not be caught out financially, she thought. Checkbook, cash, and passport. Extra insurance for loss of luggage, time, personal injury, just in case. Followed by maps, instructions, repair kit, first-aid box. An expanding bag or two would not go amiss, and the backpack and shopping bag and. . . .

What a weight to carry, she thought, but kept stacking. She packed for the weather she expected, the enjoyment she craved, the "image" to be created. Of course the emotional and psychological baggage packed itself automatically. It was all in there, past experiences and learned strategies. Fears from yesterday's wounds and failures, bad memories and good ones.

Genesis 37:1–4

Jacob settled in the land where his father had lived as an alien, the land of Canaan. This is the story of the family of Jacob.

Joseph, being seventeen years old, was shepherding the flock with his brothers; he was a helper to the sons of Bilhah and Zilpah, his father's wives; and Joseph brought a bad report of them to their father. Now Israel loved Joseph more than any other of his children, because he was the son of his old age; and he made him a long robe with sleeves. But when his brothers saw that their father loved him more than all his brothers, they hated him, and could not speak peaceably to him.

Joseph gathered a heavy burden of luggage early in life. A favorite child with the privileges and the jealousies which come with such a position. A spoiled child with a great deal more than a many-colored coat, but the coat didn't help the situation, as such a garment, in the culture of the day, denoted favor which was normally the right of the eldest son. Then, to add insult to injury, the favoritism nurtured in him an arrogance, detestable to his brothers. At seventeen he was "sneaking" to his father about their behavior. His journey of life burdened him early with some very heavy luggage indeed.

Traveler, as we step out toward Bethlehem this year it is good to take time to examine what is packed in the old suitcase. Items hidden there from years of hurts and wounds and jealousies and anger and unforgiveness. We need to cleanse our expectations of the journey, open ourselves to God's itinerary, relinquish our "image" of ourselves, whether that be good or bad. Joseph wasn't planning to go anywhere; as far as he was concerned, he'd arrived! Will our traveler begin her Advent journey making the same mistake?

Dear God, it's hard to prepare for the journey with a fresh spirit.
Been here before, we think.
Lord God, ruffle my packing enough to help me see the vision
you have for me along the way.
Please gift me with the right amount of wonder for anticipation,
a healthy degree of trepidation to know I travel
in the hands of a living God
who can touch my yesterdays as much as my tomorrows.
Lord, make me expectant, make me new. Amen.

Week 1: Monday
EXPECTATIONS
Genesis 37:5–11

His brothers said to him, "Are you indeed to reign over us? Are you indeed to have dominion over us?" So they hated him even because of his dreams and his words.

He had another dream, and told it to his brothers, saying, "Look, I have had another dream: the sun, the moon, and eleven stars were bowing down to me." But when he told it to his father and to his brothers, his father rebuked him, and said to him, "What kind of dream is this that you have had? Shall we indeed come, I and your mother and your brothers, and bow to the ground before you?" So his brothers were jealous of him, but his father kept the matter in mind.

Bigheaded or not, a dream's a dream for all that! Young Joseph, unaware of his own arrogance or of what God could do with him and through him in the future, dreamed his dreams. In them he was the hero and the sky was the limit. Like most youngsters his idealism and sense of adventure were both swashbuckling and outrageous. They made him more enemies than friends and the hatred from his brothers deepened. But God was not absent, even from the dreams. Something would have to be done with the arrogance and pride, but then God could handle that later. Meantime the maker of all things had marked the boy out for greatness and was even then preparing him for the task ahead. Before Joseph was sent on his unexpected journey, God allowed him his dreams.

Our traveler heard many people express their expectations as they packed their cases for the twenty-first century. Some dreamed of peace of mind; release from worry; freedom from fear. "Happiness," that much-defined and yet elusive Western concept of glitter and tinsel, was mentioned often. Others were depressed in the weeks preceding Christmas, imagining that everyone else in the world would be having a great time except them. It was an easy mistake to make, with all the surrounding razzamatazz of media and commerce projecting such an image. Many others would drag their steps to Bethlehem with hearts full of grief and loss, the memories of pain and suffering, walking in the loneliness of despair. Our traveler would need to remember Joseph's journey with his deep sense of betrayal and injustice. The violence and victimization perpetrated upon him by the sin of jealousy, even his father rebuking his expectations. Yet his earthly father "kept the matter in mind." Jacob, who had attempted, by deceit, to force God's hand in his earlier life, must have feared that his favorite son was a "chip off the old block" in more ways than one. Yet Jacob, now a godly man of prayer, must also have asked himself, "Where are these dreams coming from?"

Will our traveler seek God's expectations for this journey regardless of feelings or fears? Will she pack in the case tools for adventure, a camera to record the heroic deeds for the photo album upon her return? Or can she remember to pack the pickax for the hard climb up the steep slopes? The heavy boots for the deep snowfalls? The strong rope for hanging over the edge of the precipice? Adventures can be dangerous as well as exciting. Knees get scuffed, bones break, not to mention hearts.

God lets us dream our dreams as we pack the case. Expectation is half the fun of the holiday, but we must set off with a willingness to take whatever comes. Instead of asking for our heart's desire on the journey, how about asking God, "What do I need, Lord? What do you have for me on the journey? Give me what you decide." It doesn't make the traveling less exciting, it makes it more so, and a great deal safer on the sharp bends and twists of life.

Dear God, whatever my expectation I face disappointment.
Being human and a sinner,
I dream of perfect solutions and unconditional love.
I'm on the wrong planet, Lord, this one's broken,
and all my expectations are based on ideals which no one
has ever reached, except—except Jesus.
What's that you said, Lord? "The one who believes in me ... will
do greater works than these" (John 14:12)
and "I come that they may have life, and have it abundantly"
(John 10:10).
So these dreams are from you, Lord!
Life—now there's an expectation to have on the way to Bethlehem.
But what does it mean?
Lord, I'm going to fail if I try to set the agenda
or demand the outcome.
Please mold my expectations by your hand.
Lord God, as your child I expect nothing but your love,
and that is everything! Amen.

P.S. God—This year, help me look forward,
not to a perfect Christmas, but to a God-given one.
If my dream fails, help me to be the one to bring hope,
and fun, and peace
to those around me, regardless, in Jesus' name.

Week 1: Tuesday
"SOUL-NAPPED"
Genesis 37:12–14a, 17b–20

Now his brothers went to pasture their father's flock near Shechem. And Israel said to Joseph, "Are not your brothers pasturing the flock at Shechem? Come, I will send you to them." He answered, "Here I am." So he said to him, "Go now, see if it is well with your brothers and with the flock; and bring word back to me."

... So Joseph went after his brothers, and found them at Dothan. They saw him from a distance, and before he came near to them, they conspired to kill him. They said to one another, "Here comes this dreamer. Come now, let us kill him and throw him into one of the pits; then we shall say that a wild animal has devoured him, and we shall see what will become of his dreams."

Ever felt trapped? Joseph seems to have had no idea he was walking into an ambush the day his father sent him to see if his brothers were doing well.

"Here comes this dreamer," they said. Their intention was murder and the motive was clear: it was jealousy. "We shall see what becomes of his dreams," they said. They could kidnap the boy but they could never destroy intentions that were designed by God. Life was about to change utterly and very dramatically for Joseph and the journey was about to take a very strange direction indeed. He would need that soul link to God if ever he was to reach the destination of God's choosing.

Ever felt "soul-napped"? All other aspects of your life are functioning normally. Your body and mind working well for the shopping, and the driving of the children to school, or for the managerial job. The tight timetables are efficiently handled and even the golf gets played well. You're quite successful at most things, but your soul is—well, somehow it has been ambushed along the way and you're not sure when or how. You are coping very well at one level of your life but, in the inner depths of your being, you feel "soul-napped."

The road to Bethlehem should carry signposts at regular intervals marked, "Beware of ambush." Travelers journey in danger of being trapped by lack of time for prayer. No space for contemplation. Fewer and fewer moments to walk with a living God or the strength and determination to cultivate the art of listening until we perceive the drumming of God's heartbeat louder than our own. A closed Bible and a full timetable soul-naps more travelers than most bandits of secular mode.

God reaches out to introduce us to that part of our innermost being that is capable of feeling the touch of a living God. It's not merely about "having soul." Not about smelling roses and appreciating rainbows, about starry nights and warm, furry feelings in the stomach. It's not merely about walking barefoot on the grass (although that can't hurt sometimes), it's more about that which is capable of rendezvous with the Spirit's wind that blows where it wills (John 3:8). That part of us which longs to be one with the Lord if only this old earthly "flesh tent" in which we move around didn't get in the way. Our traveler might, if she thought about it, stop packing her case for a moment and listen to the sounds of God in heaven talking about the journey and the obstacles, and the highway laws and the difficulties and the promises of his guidance; and most of all the Lord would tell her of the wonderful sights and sounds and smells along the way and the chats they would enjoy together at the pit stops.

Our traveler is getting a little hesitant now. The old knees are beginning to twinge as she hunkers beside her case at her packing. Walking, like Joseph, across the unknown "no man's land" of a lifetime in which none of us knows what is around the corner. We can neither predict with certainty nor dictate with authority the outcome of a single day. But we can place our moments, step-by-step, in trustworthy hands. The Lord has us here for a purpose and our experiences, placed in the Lord's hands, can lead us to a place of rejoicing. Other years a pretty children's nativity play and a few carols constituted the journey to Bethlehem. This year, the traveler suspects, it might take more of her than she yet knows exists. But she is willing to journey, whatever the cost.

Is she?

Dear God, free my soul to journey today.
Shackled and handcuffed as it feels from chores, and duties,
and things left unforgiven, and joys left unembraced,
and sins left unconfessed, bad habits ignored and good ones uncultivated.
Lord, show me the color and substance of my soul,
and help me release it from bondage that it may soar on wings to you.
Help me prepare it with your word, the Bible.
Immerse it in prayer for cleansing.
I place it in your hands, unworthy though it is to travel. Amen.

P.S. God—Thanks for the memories, every good Christmas and bad.
For you were not absent in any of them.
Even when I feel "soul-napped" you are neither blindfolded,
nor impotent, in your forward planning.
Give me confidence that you will walk with me toward
Bethlehem this year desiring only to bless. I open myself to you.
Lord, touch, in Jesus' name.

23

Week 1: Wednesday
GOD'S PACKING
Genesis 37:21–24, 26–27

But when Reuben heard it, he delivered him out of their hands, saying, "Let us not take his life." Reuben said to them, "Shed no blood; throw him into this pit here in the wilderness, but lay no hand on him"—that he might rescue him out of their hand and restore him to his father. So when Joseph came to his brothers, they stripped him of his robe, the long robe with sleeves that he wore; and they took him and threw him into a pit. The pit was empty; there was no water in it.

. . .Then Judah said to his brothers, "What profit is it if we slay our brother and conceal his blood? Come, let us sell him to the Ishmaelites, and not lay our hands on him, for he is our brother, our own flesh."

In the frantic activity of all this case-packing let's have a break and close the lid for a moment while we think what else might have been forgotten. I don't know about you, but I tend to do a great deal of packing as late as midnight on the night before I leave for a journey. Usually it's because, in my demanding and exciting ministry travels, I often have to be ready for the road at a moment's notice. However, once in a while, I confess, it's because I have left it to the last minute, not deliberately, but due to the pressure of all those loose ends to be tied up before I go.

On these occasions I stand tired and brain-dead at the witching hour, staring at my bedside lamp, desperately trying to remember what I cannot possibly live without in order not to forget something vital. Such an exercise usually galvanizes me into a flurry of activity, from wardrobe, to chest of drawers, to bathroom cabinet, to bookcase, in a frantic attempt to gather the essentials. It ends with me in gales of exhausted laughter on the edge of my bed when the truth dawns on me that, if the plane went down, or the boat sank, or the car conked out, I'd have to do without any of it and without a lot more besides and God laughs with me and I feel God say, "Hilary, you have what you need—trust me."

Joseph, even at the very beginning of his worst nightmare, already had what he needed. God had provided him with a brother Reuben to make sure that his life was spared and a brother Judah to act as a channel to ensure that his life was twice saved and to direct his journey toward Egypt. God even ensured that there was no water in the pit into which he was thrown.

The outcome of Joseph's journey to Egypt was far-reaching, not merely for himself, but for his family and for the Israelites. He suffered great indignity, pain and imprisonment and God remolded him into a new man. A man who emerged in years to come as a great leader and deliverer in his exile, saving many people from starvation and death, not the least of whom were the very people who once planned his downfall, his own brothers.

While poor Joseph must have been feeling God's absence intensely in that pit, his Lord in heaven was working unsparingly to accomplish wonderful purposes of which Joseph had not the slightest inkling. The boy was thrust unwillingly into his journey, blindfolded in more ways than one.

Our traveler has chosen the Advent journey and is not blindfolded. From previous years the destination is known—perhaps from many years of familiar and loved traversing of the path. She has what she needs to make the journey, God has seen to that. Does she fully understand how much God is working to bring her to the manger? Does she trust the Lord to surprise her along the way? Is there a willingness to be open to a new experience of an old, traditional path, and to see it as though the journey is for the first time?

Dear God, lead me by a new way to Bethlehem,
even if the path is strewn with unexpected obstacles and challenges.
Open my eyes to see the signposts of your love
and be obedient to your commands along the way.
Thank you that the choice is mine to travel,
yet my feet are unsure, and my eyes cannot see
more than a brief step ahead.
Who is that who walks in front?
My eyes strain
to see—yes, I think, yes—thank you, God, it's you. Amen.

P.S. God—Drain the water from the pit for me.
Thank you that you have made provision
for my escape to holiness and health.
Be with me in the pit stops, Lord, in Jesus' name.

Week 1: Thursday
PREPARED
Exodus 12:11–13
(Read from the beginning of the chapter)

This is how you shall eat it: your loins girded, your sandals on your feet, and your staff in your hand; and you shall eat it hurriedly. It is the passover of the LORD. For I will pass through the land of Egypt that night, and I will strike down every firstborn in the land of Egypt, both human beings and animals; on all the gods of Egypt I will execute judgments: I am the LORD.

From Joseph to Moses is not such a great leap. They both traveled light—the first man because he was taken by surprise and by force; the second was carefully briefed by God and told to be ready, with girded loins, feet shod, staff in hand, eating in haste. God had prepared a way of escape for the chosen people. The journey of hope and faith was about to begin afresh, but to reach the promised land they also had to be prepared to travel light.

How far would I get today with what I could carry on my back, with just sandals and a walking stick to help me? Not far, I think. But I learn from this passage much more than the futility of loading ourselves down with this world's clutter, true though that is. My attention is focused on the mental image of a huge nation of slaves, in bondage for many years, standing in the dark watches of one night, holding their small children by the hand and in their arms, and slung on the women's backs in hut after hut across the rough ground of slave dwellings. Gulping down, as they stand, a quick snack of freshly slaughtered roast lamb at nightfall, with unleavened bread and bitter herbs, knowing it might be their last meal for a very long time. Worse, it might be their last meal. Forbidden by God even to pack sandwiches for the journey—eat it all or burn the leftovers, they were told. There was to be no suitcase on this journey. The object was escape and God would do the rest.

Can we travel to Bethlehem in perfect trust? No guarantees, no insurance policies of an easy journey? Either we make the climb without a safety net, or we will find at life's destination that we have never left the dull security of bondage whatever form that slavery takes. Whether it be the comfort of home, the complacency of the familiar, the luxury of unchallenged habits, the safety of self-centered living. Allowing life to dribble us like a soccer ball, gently and dangerously into a goal not of our choosing, never submitting to the changed life of God's mighty enablement. Never visiting the stable, finding the child, or discovering the truth of the cross. Never experiencing the joy of Jesus' and our own resurrection.

Our traveler will discover that the promised land does indeed flow with milk and honey but the journey toward it is through the wilderness, not amongst the fleshpots of Egypt.

On the way to Bethlehem—this year, can we stand ready with only what we carry on our backs, the traveler's cloak, sandals, stick? Can we trust the Lord for sustenance and stamina and direction? God sent a cloud by day and fire by night to lead the Israelites. We will have what we need if we follow what God sends.

The traveler prepares to open her eyes fearlessly, focusing on both the cloud and fire in her life and afraid of neither. She must see all as a challenge to journey, to launch forth, as we say in my part of the globe, "with what we stand up in." To move in vulnerability along the path of God's will and refuse to put any priority above that of encounter with, and obedience to, Jesus.

Dear God, you know the way.
You know my needs.
You know my route of escape.
May I accept no enslavement, by material possessions,
or the bondage of fear,
or the mastery of past sins or mistakes.

God, forgive me if I ever build my sense of security
upon anyone but you or anything other than
your unchanging love. All else is only on loan to me,
even those whom I love. Stand me ready at my front door,
obedient to your will, prepared for whatever
the journey may bring. Amen.

P.S. God—Thank you for the safety of your love.
For your gentle understanding.
For the challenge of the journey,
and the vision of the promised destination.
Lead me on, in Jesus' name.

Week 1: Friday
FLIES IN THE OINTMENT
Exodus 16:1–5

The whole congregation of the Israelites set out from Elim; and Israel came to the wilderness of Sin, which is between Elim and Sinai, on the fifteenth day of the second month after they had departed from the land of Egypt. The whole congregation of the Israelites complained against Moses and Aaron in the wilderness. The Israelites said to them, "If only we had died by the hand of the LORD in the land of Egypt, when we sat by the fleshpots and ate our fill of bread; for you have brought us out into this wilderness to kill this whole assembly with hunger."

Then the LORD said to Moses, "Behold, I am going to rain bread from heaven for you, and each day the people shall go out

and gather enough for that day. In that way I will test them,
whether they will follow my instruction or not. On the sixth day,
when they prepare what they bring in, it will be twice as much as
they gather on other days."

It's amazing how an experience of material discomfort can make a person, or a nation, forget everything but his stomach. God had not promised it would be easy. They knew it would be a hard trek. Hadn't they already been freed from the beatings and scourgings, the backbreaking agony of unremitting, unrewarded toil, the ignominy of watching their children born into slavery, bondaged from the womb? Without rights or privileges and with a chief expectation of dying in chains, serving human masters who could take their lives at a whim and still be within their legal rights.

The chosen children of God had sprinkled the blood on the doorpost. They had heard the mourning cries in the houses they had fled past as the firstborn male of every Egyptian household was found dead. They walked out of Egypt with their eldest sons and their entire families safe and whole. They even witnessed the horses and chariots of Pharaoh sink below the waters while they stood on dry land. God had sweetened the water for them when they were thirsty. Then the Lord had brought them rest and refreshment in the oasis of Elim. It was only fifteen days after their miraculous escape and already they had forgotten why they had been glad to run. Never mind the promised land, never mind freedom, never mind God's mercy and faithfulness, they wanted to go back to slavery. Why? Quite simply, they were hungry. How quickly we forget. Real deprivation and torture easily pale into insignificance when starvation stares us in the face.

What is the cost of the journey? Are we prepared to "rough it" for truth? Do we long for escape into a "virtual reality" world where everything comes to us at the push of a button, or can we become masters of reality? Can we see all the "flies in the ointment" transformed into opportunities to recognize the hand of God at work in a mighty way to bring good from our worst nightmares? Around the corner, for the Israelites, there were manna and quails and the patience of an all-seeing, all-loving God who knew their needs even before hearing their complaints and who had already taken steps to meet those needs in advance of the problem. Yet I've found, in my own experience, that the needs are never met beforetime. Apparently it is necessary to experience the problem before I can grow and before I can fully appreciate the meeting of that need. The manna was for each day only, not a deep freezerful for a month. Those who tried to save themselves the future toil of gathering, or escape the command to trust God for tomorrow, found the food stale and putrid. Except on the Sabbath when there was enough left over and still fresh to allow the proper worship and the proper keeping of the Lord's day.

Our traveler must journey in trust. Each day's provision for each day's need and our part is to trust and obey. Obedience with trust: these are twin items for the suitcase that are really worth their weight in gold.

Lord God, I'm hungry;
show me the food you have prepared for me.
I'm lonely;
show me the company you wish me to keep.
I'm tired;
rest me in your will.

Thank you for letting me complain sometimes
and for understanding my human weakness of needs and drives.
But, Lord, please don't let any of my needs
ever blind me to your promises.
I remember what you have done for me in the past.
Help me in my remembrance that I may never fail to trust. Amen.

P.S. God—What if I don't like the taste of manna?
Sorry, no, no, I don't want to go back to Egypt.
Stimulate new taste buds in me, Lord, in Jesus' name.

Week 1: Saturday
MORE OF GOD'S PACKING
Exodus 16:11–15

The LORD spoke to Moses and said, "I have heard the complaining of the Israelites; say to them, 'At twilight you shall eat meat, and in the morning you shall have your fill of bread; then you shall know that I am the LORD your God.'"

In the evening quails came up and covered the camp; and in the morning there was a layer of dew around about the camp. When the layer of dew lifted, there on the surface of the wilderness was a fine flaky substance, as fine as frost on the ground. When the Israelites saw it, they said to one another, "What is it?" For they did not know what it was. Moses said to them, "It is the bread that the LORD has given you to eat."

Can you imagine a hungry man not recognizing food or a starving person nourishment? God had already provided for them time and time again through the biblical history of the Israelites. God had promised this particular group of "escapees" provision for their every need. God told Moses what he would send, when he would send it, and how they were to gather it, and when it arrived they said, "What is it?" Sounds like a script for a television comedy sketch. But it just wasn't funny. Not to these poor, frightened, hungry, exhausted human beings whose faith stretched only as far as the next meal ticket.

Twenty-first-century men and women, sitting at their computers with the central heating and double-glazed windows bolstering their complacency, dare not sit in judgment on their reactions.

We ask instead whether the elasticity of our faith is as thin. Are we surrounded by the Lord's provision without knowing what it is? Feeling inadequate for a journey to Bethlehem, do we engage in furious case-packing activity at the expense of using our eyes to observe again what God is doing in all that is around us— our home, our health, our professional responsibilities, our hopes and fears, our needs and daily concerns? God says, "You shall know that I am the Lord your God."

Knowing God requires also that we become unafraid to know ourselves. Approaching almost a quarter of a century of full-time service and pastoral ministry for God, I recall, times without number, the agony of a would-be follower of Jesus whose only strategy for living was to run away, and another who could not face examining his own motivations, and a third who never reached Bethlehem or Calvary for fear of what she might discover on the journey.

God seeks each one more fervently than we can ever seek God. The Lord has quails and manna waiting, yes, and blistering sun and scorching desert too. But how can we know God's trustworthiness without stepping out in faith on the journey? How can we appreciate God's provision without the experience of hunger? How can we enjoy freedom without first having identified the sin of negativism which once held us bound?

For our traveler the case is packed and stands ready at the door. Will she have the faith and courage to step outside?

At the height of the troubles in Northern Ireland, I had to journey often between various regions in the UK and had to answer the same questions many times at a number of UK airports. The official would pick up my case and ask, "Did you pack it yourself?"

"Yes," I would reply.

"Did anyone give you anything to carry for them?" he would counter.

"No," I'd say.

"Do you know everything that is in your luggage?" he would challenge.

"Yes," I always affirmed.

The journey to Bethlehem begins. To the first question we can say, "Yes," but I doubt if any of us can be crystal clear on any of the others.

We may believe we packed it ourselves but the influences, both good and bad, of many people and many past experiences crowd into the luggage uninvited and often unknown to us. "Did anyone give you anything to carry?" It is a journey we each must make unburdened with another person's luggage. Neither can we rest upon the faith or commitment of our parents or grandparents. No one is a Christian from the womb. Our salvation is inherited only by conscious choice of surrender to Christ. For the one whom we seek in the stable wishes to address each individual profoundly, directly, one-to-one.

We cannot know everything that we carry. For better or worse we are packed and ready. The traveler moves into the hallway, picks up the luggage and turns to bid farewell to home.

Dear Lord, this feels like a heavy bag I carry.
I don't know why it should weigh a ton.
I wanted only a few of my most precious possessions—
sorry, of your precious possessions. I can't go empty-handed.
Lord, surely you wouldn't want me to turn up empty-handed—
would you? Amen.

P.S. God—Thank you for your promise
that your yoke is easy and your burden is light.
Help me jettison all else, in Jesus' name.

SAYING GOOD-BYE

Week 2

Week 2: Sunday
FOCUSING THE EYE
Matthew 6:19–23

Do not store up for yourselves treasures on earth, where moth and rust consume and where thieves break in and steal; but store up for yourselves treasures in heaven, where neither moth nor rust consumes and where thieves do not break in and steal. For where your treasure is, there will your heart be also.

The eye is the lamp of the body. So, if your eye is healthy, your whole body will be full of light; but if your eye is unhealthy, your whole body will be full of darkness. If then the light in you is darkness, how great is the darkness!

Good-byes are never easy. We cling to the familiar as a drowning man grasps a straw. The preparation for taking leave of a familiar situation is usually aided a little by all those last-minute chores that have to be done before we can venture forth. The milk and papers to be canceled, the cat-sitter to be organized, the kennels to be booked. But sooner or later, like it or not, we stand in the hall and that awful farewell has to be said. Will the house be safe? If there is a burglar alarm, will it work? Can we trust the neighbors to keep an eye on everything? Did we lock the back door? Are the windows shut? It's at moments like these that we truly discover the degree of attachment we have developed to our possessions, material and otherwise. Our eye falls on our most cherished items, and people, and we fear to part from them.

The eye, says Jesus, is where we have to start in preparing to journey toward him. Like the small boy who, when leaving a children's party without saying thank you to his hostess, was asked, "Haven't you forgotten something?" He stopped and looked back at the still-laden table of goodies, then, without a glance at the hostess, he ran back in and stuffed his pockets full of buns before rushing through the door.

What is in the traveler's eye as she bids farewell on the way to Bethlehem? Can she take her gaze from the dazzling array of goodies seductively arranged for the shopper as Christmas approaches? Can she help her loved ones, big and little, to do the same? Can alternative gifts be endowed from head and heart, instead of purse and wallet? Gifts of time given to the unlovely, gifts of tolerance shown at a moment of anger, peace for frustration, forgiveness for evil done toward her, compassion offered for the negative retort. While others run back to grab an extra bun on leaving, can she let her eye focus upon the host at the table, Jesus, and thank the Lord, not merely for the goodies but for what Jesus did to give us something to celebrate?

Turning backward, what other sights are cherished—accumulated wealth of knowledge, religious observance, denominational pride, traditional rites? Can the turning be beyond all of these, and focus instead on the search for the biblical child, the promised Messiah about to be born in a stable and laid in a manger? Is it possible to travel empty of pocket and open of heart to Bethlehem? Beyond tinsel-laden, aromatic shops in commercial malls, family demands, work pressures, telephone jangle and that unresolved problem that will not go away, will the traveler identify a need, a hunger to learn more of Christ?

When I was a child I was taught, "Where the eye looks, the feet will follow." Now there's good navigational advice for the journey! As we say good-bye to all our need for security and the pretty, valuable, and well-loved items adorning our past, we look toward a new dawning. A day when Jesus' face will be more desirable to our eyes than gold or silver; Jesus' truth more precious than wealth or power; Jesus' love more fulfilling than anything designed, sold or bartered on earth.

Lord God Almighty, I'm leaving soon.
Leaving the old desires, the old wants and wants and wants.
Put the desire in me for only those things that you desire
me to know and to have and to love.
Jesus, my eye is so clouded by the pressures and demands
of the dark surroundings of this world.
Show me the light of your Bible truth.
Show me yourself,
even as I pick up the courage
to say good-bye to
all my past longings and desires. Amen.

P.S. God—Thanks that life can be lived
in simplicity without austerity, can be taken seriously without
dire solemnity or oppression by that which is shabby.
Thank you that the Lord who wore a homespun cloak
was son to the God who created the fabulous colors of the rainbow.
Color me joyful, in Jesus' name.

Week 2: Monday
FOCUSING THE PAIN
Psalm 22:14–21

> *I am poured out like water,*
>   *and all my bones are out of joint;*
> *my heart is like wax,*
>   *it is melted within my breast;*
> *my mouth is dried up like a potsherd,*
>   *and my tongue sticks to my jaws;*
> *you lay me in the dust of death.*
>
> *For dogs are all around about me;*
>   *a company of evildoers encircles me.*
> *My hands and feet have shriveled;*
>   *I can count all my bones.*
> *They stare and gloat over me;*
>   *they divide my clothes among themselves,*
> *and for my clothing they cast lots....*
>
> *Deliver my soul from the sword,*
>   *my life from the power of the dog!*
> *Save me from the mouth of the lion!*
>
> *From the horns of the wild oxen....*

David's cry of anguish is extremely graphic. There is nothing vague about his expression of loss. He had been deprived of family and praise and a position of privilege, had suffered reversal of love to hate, once being the king's favorite. He had lost a beloved friend, Jonathan, and all his dreams and ambitions had turned into a nightmare as he fled for his life, hiding in caves and wilderness places.

Did he get time to say good-bye to all of this? Probably not. It's not a passage which would normally spring to mind in thoughts of Advent. But no journey can be undertaken, Advent or otherwise, without recognizing where we are now. In this psalm David is expressing deep grief because all loss is a bereavement. His grief is specific. He cites every part of his being in his effort to heal the pain.

"Poured out like water." Does our traveler feel that terrible helplessness of loss at the start of her journey, this year? As though the precious life force within has spilled, wasted upon the ground?

"Bones out of joint." Does every bone ache with the force of the grief and the weight of it?

"My heart is like wax." Love melted and wasted, too hurt to ever risk loving again?

"Mouth dried up." Hard, brittle, cracked surface of weakness, with no hope of recovery?

David feels at the mercy of forces worse than human. He feels attacked by animalistic threats—dogs, lions, wild oxen. With what graphic imagery he portrays his sense of loss and hurt, fear and desolation! His very soul is threatened by his experience of pain.

Anticipating Christmas and New Year can be the hardest time for many who have suffered loss, or who endure loneliness or persecution. The "slap it on quick and be brave" face is more helpful to the observer than to the owner-occupier of such a mask. Whether the grief is from loss of a loved one, betrayal by a friend, loss of employment, home, security, or loss of hope itself, the pain is real and devastating, and God knows it.

Half the battle is being able to focus for a temporary period on that pain and acknowledge it for what it is, refusing to deny what we are feeling on our way to Bethlehem this year. David took steps to deal with the pain.

He faced it and, without denial, expressed it fully. At the beginning of the psalm he tells God exactly how he feels. He pulls no punches.

Then he remembers what God's nature is and what God has already done for his people. He remembers God's consistency and love and puts his trust in the Lord.

On preparing to leave, our traveler invites Christ to purge body, mind and soul from the negative effects of past debilitating suffering. We cannot live a pain-free life, not on a broken planet, but we can come to know and to say, "This is how it was, and this is how it is just now. I may have to sit within the pain for a while, but it does not have to stay like this forever."

God has touched it, things can change. By the power of the living God, they will change.

Dear God, I don't want to focus on the pain.
It hurts too badly.
I'd rather pretend it isn't so, "water off a duck's back."
But I don't want to carry this with me all the way to Bethlehem.
Help me say good-bye to the pain,
not by leaving it behind, but by facing it
and allowing you inside it to transform and to heal.
Bid it farewell with me, Lord.
When I allow you to do that
I see it flee from me like phantoms in the light of day.

Already the luggage feels a little lighter
as I step along the passage. Thank you.

P.S. God—Thank you that if I lose everything I still have Jesus.
Jesus is all I have, Jesus is all I need. Thank you, Lord.

Week 2: Tuesday
FOCUSING THE HEART
Ezekiel 11:17–20

Therefore say: Thus says the Lord GOD: I will gather you from the
peoples, and assemble you out of the countries where you have been
scattered, and I will give you the land of Israel. When they come there,
they will remove from it all its detestable things and all its abomina-
tions. I will give them one heart, and put a new spirit within them;
I will take the heart of stone from their flesh and give them a heart
of flesh, so that they may follow my statutes and keep my ordinances
and obey them. Then they shall be my people, and I will be their God.

What a promise from God! "I will give them one heart, and put
a new spirit within them." Just imagine having new heart put
back in your life. A spirit free and lightened from the burdens and
fears and enslavement which threaten so much of life on earth.
What a promise for the journey. Every promise of God comes
with an accompanying command. Often we read in the Bible
God promising, "If you will do this . . . then I will do this. . . ."

Not that God bargains with us. It's not a bargain, it's a revelation to show us which plant grows from which seed. Here

Ezekiel hears that the seed of repentance, the removal of "all its detestable things and all its abominations," will restore Israel. The evidence of real repentance will result in unity of heart and a new spirit. Repentance is the seed, new heart and spirit are the fruit—and what a harvest and restoration resulted for God's people! We wish to journey toward Bethlehem. For the success of this journey we take time first to repent of past journeys to wrong destinations.

The traveler had canceled the milk and the papers. She had said good-bye to the neighbors and they had promised to keep an eye on the house while she was away; but saying good-bye to the heart's previous attitudes and fears, this would be hard.

Focusing the heart and spirit for the renewed touch of God cannot be accomplished without repentance. Those who feel quite good enough to worship at the manger will never truly leave the safety of home, no matter how many miles they cover.

She knew that without deep repentance the journey to the stable would be in vain. She focused upon each element of her life and laid it open before the Lord. Jesus took her painful offerings so tenderly and showed her that repentance is more than regret, it is more than confession, it goes deeper than sorrow itself. When Ezekiel led the people to repentance he did not line them up in long lines and ask them to say they were sorry to God. He watched as they emptied their houses and their homes of all that was not God. Every false idol, every pagan desire, every perversion of the truth of God in scripture.

They prepared for the promises of God by ridding themselves of all but God. Only when there was nothing left but God could they experience all that God was. Our traveler said good-bye to every particle of life that was not God's will, God's morals, God's ethics. Everything that was not an expression of the Lord's love had to be left behind. She knew it was the work of more than a day or a week. Saying good-bye to the old heart would take patience and practice and a large amount of God's grace.

Dusting in the dark corners of mind and soul we find things that were never in the mind of Christ. Only Christ can help us walk away from these dust traps. Before we bid farewell to home, clear out the cupboards and focus the heart on repentance and cleansing. God will help with the farewells. God knows how hard it is living as a human being. God calls us to come without fear, so that he can put a new spirit within.

Dear God, give us heart for the journey, we pray.
Not the one broken by pride, handcuffed by pain,
stinted by sin and fear.
But a humbled heart, forgiven and forgiving.
Fearless in the fight for truth and in the service of
all those broken people whom we pass along the way to Bethlehem.
Put heart into our step, a new heart, Lord, we pray. Amen.

P.S. God—Thank you for your understanding of brokenness,
for experiencing it yourself.
I see the shattered pieces of life,
as you gently reassemble them in your hands.
They rest upon the marks of the nail prints on your palms.
They belong there, in Jesus' name.

Week 2: Wednesday
FOCUSING THE MIND
1 Corinthians 4:9–13

*For I think that God has exhibited us apostles as last of all, as though
sentenced to death, because we have become a spectacle to the world, to
angels and to mortals. We are fools for the sake of Christ, but you are
wise in Christ. We are weak, but you are strong. You are held in honor,
but we in disrepute. To the present hour we are hungry and thirsty, we
are poorly clothed and beaten and homeless, and we grow weary from
the work of our own hands. When reviled, we bless; when persecuted,
we endure; when slandered, we speak kindly. We have become like the
rubbish of the world, the dregs of all things, to this very day.*

In the wisdom of hindsight, what changes would you make to life?
What mistakes would you correct? What decisions might you
reverse? On the verge of leaving we must bid farewell to the world's
wisdom. Like the small boy who was asked by a sage, wise in the
world's eyes, which of the birds hidden in his hands was alive or
dead. The child, wishing to pass the test and be seen as wise at the
start of his apprenticeship, wrestled in his mind to seek the correct
answer. Was the man's right hand holding the live bird or his left
hand? Then, with great insight the child realized that the man
could squeeze the neck of either of the birds at will, and the child
replied, "Whichever hand decides to kill, in that hand lies the dead
bird." The man opened his palms and both birds flew away, alive.
The boy, considering that the sage had been prepared to kill a live
bird in the interest of wisdom, left that place and refused to work
in the man's tutelage. He chose to become foolish by the criteria

of worldly wisdom, and by doing so he attained a wisdom and a compassion greater than the sage himself.

Paul's life had been turned upside down when he met the risen Christ on the road to Damascus. All measure of intellect and ambition and social status and national pride became surrendered to the higher criteria of Christ's commands and teaching.

His new behavior and priorities and concerns were the antithesis of what had once seemed wise according to his previously held earthly values.

On the face of it he was now a fool, blessing those who did him wrong, forgiving his enemies, while those around him met every slight with attempts at revenge, used "might is right" tactics. Even some of the churches to which he wrote seemed to display all the symptoms of arrogance and the world's wisdom.

Saying good-bye to our old ways of arrogance and pride and the reasoning of the world around us is not easy, especially when the pressure to conform screams at us from every billboard and magazine and TV advertisement. When every interview situation, or party encounter, or the professional criteria of our employment, threatens to push us along a road that leads to everywhere except Bethlehem, it is difficult to focus the mind on the journey. We travel with the mind of Christ or we journey elsewhere.

The traveler, wishing to focus her wisdom for the journey, visualized all the aspects of her life competing for her attention—present concerns; daily pressures; fears for the future. Like vulnerable birds trapped in another's hands they trembled before her, flapping their wings constantly in front of her face until she was powerless to choose which should have priority. One by one she took each demented bird and placed it into the hands of God. Some clung to God's fingers, some climbed from God's wrist to shoulder, some walked across God's chest and around the back of his neck. With great power and tolerance the Lord allowed each small bird to perch and peck and tweak at his outstretched arms and forehead but the Lord killed none of them. God allowed all to live. "It is not the birds you must put to death," God lovingly whispered, "but your fear of them." To be a fool for Christ we must journey accepting no wisdom but Christ's.

Dear Lord, I cannot change my mind,
full as it is with this world's brainwashing.
Put a new mind within me, the mind of Christ,
focused and single-minded toward Bethlehem.
Make me less fearful of being called "fool" by the world
than determined never to hear you say the words,
"I never knew you." Amen.

P.S. God—Thank you that when I need to make up my mind
you have provided the Bible for guidance,
prayer for divine communication,
and your Spirit for empowerment in every circumstance.
Focus my mind on you, in Jesus' name.

Week 2: Thursday
FOCUSING ON THE TASK
Luke 9:57–62

As they were going along the road, someone said to him, "I will follow you wherever you go." And Jesus said to him, "Foxes have holes, and birds of the air have nests; but the Son of Man has nowhere to lay his head." To another he said, "Follow me." But he said, "Lord, first let me go and bury my father." But Jesus said to him, "Let the dead bury their own dead; but as for you, go and proclaim the kingdom of God." Another said, "I will follow you, Lord; but let me first say farewell to those at my home." Jesus said to him, "No one who puts a hand to the plow and looks back is fit for the kingdom of God."

Excuses, excuses, excuses, this Bible passage is full of them. There are as many reasons for not stepping out on the journey of faith as there are cones on a highway repair job. Long lines on the road tell me I'm approaching a freshly laid transportation-department traffic trap. I must make a decision, stay at home and wait for the obstacles, and the line, to clear (maybe they will in several months or so). Or find another route (what if there isn't one?). Or say good-bye to unobstructed coasting at my self-appointed speed and follow the proper route, focusing, mile by mile, not upon the cones, but upon the task in hand, the progress toward the destination.

"Putting the hand to the plow" is not such a graphic illustration for those city folk, like myself, who are not born to the farming life. But even I can imagine the zigzag furrow which would result from a backward glance. For a driver, what about the result of constantly staring through the rearview mirror on a series of hairpin bends? Or a man marking out the lines on a football field while walking backward?

It's not too simple focusing on the task ahead when behind lies a series of demands still unmet, problems unresolved, hurts unhealed, other people's expectations unfulfilled. But we cannot walk forward while facing backward—at least not for long before we come to grief over some obstacle unseen. Our traveler steps out on the journey amidst the imminent demands of a twenty-first-century lifestyle which propagates a split-attention, shallow-concentration existence. A strobe-lighting, negative effect upon the soul which fragments contemplation and short-circuits true fulfillment. God knows about responsibilities both domestic and otherwise. Jesus certainly did not abandon his role as the eldest son, carrying on the family business as a carpenter after the death of Joseph and continuing as the chief breadwinner of the family very likely until the younger children were grown. Jesus reached thirty before launching out on public ministry and even on the cross made full provision for his mother, placing her in the trust-worthy hands of the beloved disciple, John.

It is not in abandonment of our responsibilities that we journey toward Bethlehem but in examining every demand upon us in the light of that short but devastating phrase from the lips of Jesus, "Follow me."

Our traveler knew the Lord would never call her to do anything contrary to the word of God in scripture, nor would Jesus' call ever place in jeopardy those beloved ones gifted to her by Jesus' own loving designs. Excuses not to journey spiritually can come in all shapes and sizes—too busy, ineptitude, complacency—but as in the case of the wise men, a star requires the search. Like Zacchaeus, the view over the heads of the world's crowded thoroughfares requires the effort to scramble up a tree. Like Jesus, forty days in a wilderness make for hunger and thirst and lead to a cross, but the end result—think of the result!

"Follow me," says Jesus, and if we are not sure where we are going, that's fine. Jesus has already been there and knows every step of the way. The task in hand is to keep our focus upon

Jesus, and the furrow can be plowed straight ahead, and glorious is the rejoicing.

> *Jesus, I look at you and I have no excuse.*
> *Nails, beatings, betrayed by your best friend*
> *and still you kept walking in your Father's will.*
> *Forgive my backward glances at security, comfort,*
> *gilt-edged family guarantees, and take me where*
> *you had in mind when you first said, "Follow me." Amen.*
> *P.S. God—Thanks that your way is "the road less traveled"*
> *and, though narrow, will make "all the difference"*
> (Robert Frost).

Week 2: Friday
GOOD-BYE ALL
Mark 10:25–31

"It is easier for a camel to go through the eye of a needle than for someone who is rich to enter the kingdom of God." They were greatly astounded and said to one another, "Then who can be saved?" Jesus looked at them and said, "For mortals it is impossible, but not for God; for God all things are possible."

Peter began to say to him, "Look, we have left everything and followed you." Jesus said, "Truly I tell you, there is no one who has left house or brothers or sisters or mother or father or children or fields, for my sake and for the sake of the good news, who will not receive a hundredfold now in this age—houses, brothers and sisters, mothers and children, and fields with persecutions—and in the age to come eternal life. But many who are first will be last, and the last will be first."

Mark suggests that the humorous story that Jesus told about a camel going through the eye of a needle (or not, as the case may be) was not created in a vacuum. The gospel writer places it in the context of an encounter Jesus had with a rich young ruler. Jesus was about to set out on a journey and a rich young man delayed him with a zealous appeal to learn more of how to inherit eternal life. Neither Matthew nor Luke records anything about a proposed journey but Mark mentions it and therefore I can't help wondering if the eager young Mark was not a little frustrated at the delay in leaving as Jesus took time to answer the rich young ruler's questions.

Our traveler was also accumulating many questions for Jesus on her journey to Bethlehem. "Why" questions, and "where to" questions and "how to" questions. Tearful and angry and scared questions. Many travelers fail to find answers to the half of them because of the fear of Jesus seeing inside their luggage, or fellow church members commenting on the state of the outside of their luggage, or fear that if they got the answers they sought, they would not be the ones they thought they were looking for.

Confused? We often are! When we ask the Lord a question, the Lord often gives an answer to a different question which we didn't know to ask. Yet when we hear it, we know that it is really the answer to every question we need to know.

It was just so for the rich young ruler. Perhaps he was even considering going with Jesus along the road if the great teacher had given him a suitable answer to his questions. What would a suitable answer have been? How about, "Yes, son, you've done your best, come with me on the journey and keep trying hard"? Or perhaps, "No one could do more than you've done already and your wealth would be a great asset to a ministry like mine"? Or maybe even, "Your enthusiasm and zeal will take you a great distance toward the destination and with my strength you can make it. Just drop in behind the other disciples and think no more about these difficult questions"? Jesus didn't say any of these, not because no grain of truth was contained in them, but because the Lord knew this young man right through to his very soul and he saw something that was too heavy a burden to allow the ruler to reach his destination. A great burdensome backpack of goodies he had accumulated and was dragging along behind him on his way through life. The young man would have had to stop constantly to make sure nothing valuable had dropped off as he journeyed. No wonder Jesus had to let the lad turn away sorrowful, although I dare say the greater sorrow was in Jesus' heart as he watched him go.

Our backpack may not be laden down with material possessions or wealth, but there are many other possessions we hold dear: people, ambitions, pride, habits or desires that need to be jettisoned. Say good-bye to all, or don't leave home until you do.

Take this, Lord, and this, and this,
and, no, not that, please, Lord, anything but. . . .
Thank you, Jesus, you took that too. Now I'm traveling!

P.S. God—I wonder what Mark felt as he and Jesus left,
late, on their journey.
Did he pray for the rich young ruler?
Did Mark jettison his impatience at the delay?

Was he angry at the ruler?
Thank you, Lord, for your patience with me.
Thank you that it is never too late to start again, until the end.
Help me to follow closer on the way, in Jesus' name.

Week 2: Saturday
THE INVISIBLE GOOD-BYE
Matthew 6:25–26, 31–34

Therefore I tell you, do not worry about your life, what you will eat or what you will drink, or about your body, what you will wear. Is not life more than food, and the body more than clothing? Look at the birds of the air; they neither sow nor reap nor gather into barns, and yet your heavenly Father feeds them. Are you not of more value than they? . . . Therefore do not worry, saying, "What will we eat?" or "What will we drink?" or "What will we wear?" For it is the Gentiles who strive for all these things; and indeed your heavenly Father knows that you need all these things. But strive first for the kingdom of God and his righteousness, and all these things will be given to you as well.

So do not worry about tomorrow, for tomorrow will bring worries of its own. Today's trouble is enough for today.

It's strange how often in literature I read about worry "stalking" someone. "Worry stalked her all her days." It never seems to know how to bid us farewell, does it? We shake its hand firmly at the door as we leave on a brand-new venture for which we are more than adequately prepared and, before we get any distance at all, there it is creeping behind like an insistent shadow. "Did we lock the back door?" "Is everything switched off?" "What have we forgotten?" "Will the kids be OK?" "Did Grandma make that doctor's appointment?" "Did the folk in the office read the instructions left on my desk for them?" "Will the car act up?" "What if? . . ."

It's a wonder how any of us ever get from birth to death at all, considering the number of "worry ambushes" lurking behind every tree on our journey through life. Jesus spoke a great deal about anxiety to the disciples, mainly in respect of getting rid of it. Jesus' advice was less about struggling to put it out of our minds than about replacing it with something else until our minds are so full of the replacement that there is no more room for the worry. That something else is God's kingdom and God's righteousness. When our total focus is on Jesus and seeing the kingdom of God grow and develop and manifest itself in our lives and behavior and attitudes, worry, while never completely banished, nevertheless becomes subservient to these higher concerns.

Our traveler had completed her packing and said her farewells but kept hearing from people who told her repeatedly not to worry. Isn't that just exactly what a pilgrim does not need to hear on the way to Bethlehem? I mean, robbers hide behind every rock, wild beasts stalk the long grass, signposts are few or turned around to send the traveler up the wrong road, not to mention boulders falling from the steep cliffs, and what do the armchair critics advise as you close the front door? "Don't worry," they say!

Can't you just imagine them advising Jesus at the start of his journey? "Well now, son, I know the stable will be uncomfortable, and Herod will be close at hand, and friends won't be much help to you, and the crowds will turn against you and there are the beatings, and a sham of a trial, and a trudge up Calvary's hill, and then at the top. . . .Well, best not to think about it—don't worry."

Jesus would never be so insensitive with us. The Lord says, "Do not worry about your life" because the Lord is in control. Jesus will waste nothing, especially not our suffering. Jesus knows what we need. It is what we seek that will define each day's victory, moment by moment.

Trust and worry cannot live in the same thought, they cancel each other out. Trust that is predominant places worry where it belongs, as an inferior urge whose only value is to ensure we take responsible precautions to lock up before we leave the house. Saying good-bye, we do what is necessary, but we leave behind the invisible specter of anxiety that threatens to cripple the heart and mind. Strength will be needed on the journey and worry only saps strength, whereas trust in the Lord empowers and energizes.

Lord God, I trust you but I'm scared.
So many pitfalls lie ahead.
"How do you know, my child?"
Well, I imagine it is so, Lord.
"Child, imagine less than you trust.
Imagination exercised to excess can strengthen the fear muscles.
Trust, on the other hand, produces muscles where
steroids cannot reach and with these muscles
we can make it all the way to the end."

P.S. God—I'm worried that I don't deserve your love.
What's that you say? I'm right, I don't.
Yet you still love me.
What am I worrying about? Thank you, Jesus.

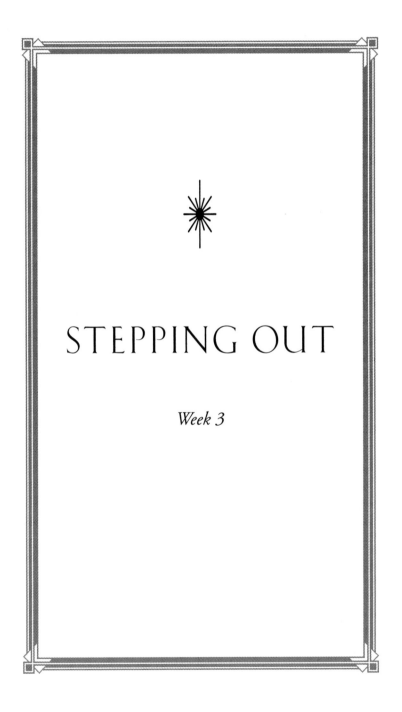

STEPPING OUT

Week 3

Week 3: Sunday
RISKING HOPE THROUGH OBEDIENCE
Luke 3:2–6

During the high priesthood of Annas and Caiaphas, the word of God came to John son of Zechariah in the wilderness. He went into all the region around the Jordan, proclaiming a baptism of repentance for the forgiveness of sins, as it is written in the book of the words of the prophet Isaiah,

> *"The voice of one crying out in the wilderness:*
> *'Prepare the way of the Lord, make his paths straight.*
> *Every valley shall be filled,*
> *and every mountain and hill shall be made low,*
> *and the crooked shall be made straight,*
> *and the rough ways shall be made smooth;*
> *and all flesh shall see the salvation of God.'"*

The ground underfoot had become sandy earlier than expected. The supplies of water had dried up more quickly than our traveler had anticipated. The sun overhead burned incessantly, so that there was no hiding place from the heat.

She heard the man's voice before she saw him. It carried a note of urgency across the wilderness through which she journeyed. In it was all the discipline of a diet of locusts and wild honey. The spartan self-denial of camel-hair cloak and thin sandals on grit-chafed feet. "Repent!" it trumpeted against the stifling air. His speech was as common as the neighboring hills but his certainty of belief and purpose was rock solid, built on the foundation of his own experience. He spoke of one who was to come after him and, listening, she knew that he was speaking of someone he knew personally.

This man had met the one whose beginning was in a stable, whose mission led him to a cross, and whose kingdom had no ending. The voice of John the Baptist helped her step out on the journey across the wilderness, taught her that such a journey was about sand in the nostrils and thirst in the back of the throat. He spoke of a great destination. A Savior who was the destination itself. Rough paths made smooth. The hope of mountains laid low, obstacles overcome, crooked places straightened. But his call was to obedience: "Repent," he said. There was to be a turning around from wrong paths, a changing of old ways. A new promised path requires a change of direction. The route to hope is by way of obedience.

He said he was just "a voice" and not the one himself who was to straighten the paths and lower the mountains. But hearing him she felt compelled to step out in response to the call to journey. He prepared the way for his Lord by suffering, by proclaiming the Lord's coming, and by eventually giving his own life that the promised one might make his own journey toward Calvary and the empty tomb.

John stretched his arms both ways. Backward toward the Old Testament in the style of all the prophets before him and forward like a bridge to the new order of things where sacrifice and righteousness would no longer be a mere matter of human effort, doomed to failure, but the certainty of Christ's perfect sacrifice to atone, to make "at one" God and man, and man and man, forever.

Do you struggle to make this journey? Life, for John, was not an existence, but a calling; not just a destination, but a preparation. It was not a burden, but a challenge. Each traveler to Bethlehem is called to walk the Lord's path and by doing so to prepare a way for the Lord's kingdom to come on earth. Our struggles and pain and frustrations are part of the process which levels hills and fills valleys for others to step more surely toward God's love and toward life more abundant. What a strange thought, to be "land-fill" for Jesus. A concept unpalatable to all but those who have the courage to risk hope through obedience.

Savior, as I step into your will, I choose the wilderness.
I embrace whatever comes as a preparation
for the treading of your way.
Please supply water in the day of thirst
and food in the famine for my spirit.
And in the noonday heat, help me toil without ceasing
as I strive to prepare the way for you.
Thank you for what you are doing with the boulders in my path,
the rough ground underfoot
and, when I come to the next hill,
please help me see it in a new light. Amen.

P.S. God—I thank you that when I look toward
Bethlehem and Calvary
I see real obedience in the behavior of Jesus.
Train me to act like Jesus, in Jesus' name.

Week 3: Monday
RISKING CLEANLINESS THROUGH TRUTH
Matthew 23:23–26

Woe to you, scribes and Pharisees, hypocrites! For you tithe mint, dill, and cummin, and have neglected the weightier matters of the law: justice and mercy and faith. It is these you ought to have practiced without neglecting the others. You blind guides! You strain out a gnat but swallow a camel!

Woe to you, scribes and Pharisees, hypocrites! For you clean the outside of the cup and of the plate, but inside they are full of greed and self-indulgence. You blind Pharisee! First clean the inside of the cup, so that the outside also may become clean.

Stepping out had been a risky business, but, as darkness fell, our traveler became less sure of her footsteps. In the growing darkness she struggled to adjust her eyesight to the gloom. "Shine a light," she prayed, "please, I need light." Her guide on the journey could not be seen but she knew he was there. She could feel his presence pacing the ground beside her step by step. "Light?" he said, "but I have no dim light." "What do you mean?" she asked. "See," he said. Immediately a pointer of light slim as a needle and bright as a laser seared the path before them and speared her to the axle of her soul.

Its light illuminated every action she had ever committed, revealing each action's motivation, naked and glistening in sharp focus. Things she had never known, never imagined about herself lay large and transparent, pulsating in the narrow beam. Like dead men's bones her moments lay rotted but refusing to decompose in the spotlight.

"Turn it off," she shouted. "I'd rather have the darkness than this terrible light."

"How shall you see the way?" asked her guide.

"I needed light, not pain," said the traveler.

"But my light is truth," said the guide. "If you walk in my light then the truth of the darkness is revealed."

She wanted to move forward. She wanted an end to the darkness. The pain was the pain of the scalpel removing cancer, the pain of the dentist's pliers closing round the offending tooth to pull until there is no more diseased tooth and no more agonizing pain.

Lord, I've done my best, like the Pharisees.
Every law has been obeyed, every observance carefully maintained.
Help me keep them, because they are not unnecessary,
they are your law and they can't be wrong.
But your light shows me the depths you are prepared to go with me,
to apply your cleansing truth.
Another law lies now within my heart
and the two are twins, not enemies.
Justice and mercy and faith, not to mention love,
What scares me, Lord, are your words that even
to think murder is to commit it.
How many times, for how many crimes,
ought I to have been in jail already?
Help shine your light this Advent, Lord.
Lighten my darkness and brighten my awareness of sin.
I want to be clean, to step forward
with hope along the way. Amen.

ADVENT MEDITATION
The Spotlight

✳

A spotlight shone onto the earth
Illuminating the darkness,
Revealing crevices and corners no one had ever seen before,
Combing the world in search of cobwebs,
Zooming in on specks of dust
So that all could see them for what they were—
Mountains of dirt.
But the people were angry,
Angry and frightened.
"Give us back our darkness," they said.
"In the darkness we didn't see the dust—we want no light."
So they destroyed that spotlight,
Snuffed it out as one would a candle.
Darkness once more!
But it was darkness with a difference.
For everywhere along the edge of the world
Appeared lights, tiny lights,
Miniature copies of the spotlight, not nearly as strong,
But each shedding tiny beams of light onto the dust.
They began to multiply—slowly,
Then faster and faster.
They were the spotlight's hope
And the spotlight was their reason for existence.
And they waited for the light.
And the light looked down upon the globe

And saw the tiny sparks of light.
Some were flickering,
Some were dim,
Some were bright as the North Star,
And in between there was darkness.
And the Light prepared to shatter that darkness—forever.

Week 3: Tuesday
RISKING LOVE
John 15:12–17

This is my commandment, that you love one another as I have loved you. No one has greater love than this, to lay down one's life for one's friends. You are my friends if you do what I command you. I do not call you servants any longer, because the servant does not know what the master is doing; but I have called you friends, because I have made known to you everything that I have heard from my Father. You did not choose me but I chose you. And I appointed you to go and bear fruit, fruit that will last, so that the Father will give you whatever you ask him in my name. I am giving you these commands so that you may love one another.

Our traveler was talking to God as she continued on her way.

"Ah yes, the love path. Well, Christmas is all about woolly lambs and cuddly babies and presents under the tree. Goodwill is everywhere and warm furry feelings in the stomach and let's not say anything too nasty to Cousin Maddy, at least not until Christmas is over. Hopefully she will go home by teatime this year.

"What's that you say, Lord? Greater love? Lay down . . . what?

"Yes, but surely you were speaking specifically about your sacrifice on the cross for us and, after all, you are God, but as for me—well, Lord, I'm sure you understand that I'm only human and . . . what? Love as you have loved? Surely you can't mean that? I mean, it's a bit extreme, isn't it? Yes, of course I'm your friend. No, I haven't changed my mind. Yes, I've every intention of making this journey.

"Couldn't I just do my very best not to hate? Well, I didn't quite mean what I said to that person yesterday. This anger is hard to control, Lord. Lose control—what do you mean?

"I must lose control to you. Oh, you mean let my anger go by telling you? No, that's not it? It's more than that? Let my will surrender until you control my love? Can you actually teach me love, Lord? You won't teach? Well, then, there is no hope because I. . . . Oh, you're saying that you can be love in me. I think I'm beginning to understand. You want to pour your love out dramatically for the world and in the world, and you have chosen to do this chiefly through your servants. Sorry, not servants, friends. Are you sure, Lord? We're not very worthy and I don't think that. . . .

"Yes, Lord, you're right, I do talk too much and listen too little. What were you saying?

"This love business is about bearing fruit for you in the world. In fact love is one of the greater fruits of your act of salvation. You loved: result—crucifixion: result—life for those who believe and follow.

"To follow is to obey. Your command is to love, and we obey. . . .

"Now I understand! We are now your love for the world and light and peace. All this Advent talk of light coming into the world means that it comes also through us!"

The shock of the realization and wonder of such a revelation stopped the traveler dead in her tracks. Here she was stumbling through the wilderness, complaining about the sand in her shoes, and God was not merely promising to light her way but asking to shine the light through her. "But I can't do it," she said. "Of course you can't," God replied. "Why do you think I came?"

"I hate to tell you this, Lord, but we're not doing too well so far. I mean, there's not a lot of light about. If only. . . .

"What's that you say? It's because I've still got control? Yes, Lord, if only I could lose control to you."

Loving you, Lord—
it's the only way.
Loving you despite the mockery and the effort
and the risk of getting hurt.
Loving you until all the pictures of woolly lambs
and butterflies give way to sacrificial love,
until we begin to smell the stench and putrid wounds
we must heal in your name.
Until we are left with the love which costs us dearly
and mirrors, in real tears of pain and joy,
the agony you knew on Calvary.
And in the same eternal moment
we find ourselves completely free.
Please, Lord, free us from ourselves in order to love. Amen.

P.S. God—While I'm trying to learn how to love,
thank you for loving me unconditionally.
Learning by example: that's how it's done, in Jesus' name.

Week 3: Wednesday
RISKING THE CROSS
Mark 8:34–38

He called the crowd with his disciples, and said to them, "If any want to become my followers, let them deny themselves and take up their cross and follow me. For those who want to save their life will lose it, and those who lose their life for my sake, and for the sake of the gospel, will save it. For what will it profit them to gain the whole world and forfeit their life? Indeed, what can they give in return for their life? Those who are ashamed of me and of my words in this adulterous and sinful generation, of them the Son of Man will also be ashamed when he comes in the glory of his Father with the holy angels."

A heavy mist had been hampering our traveler's journey, but now it began to clear a little. She was able to gather some speed for a short distance as, head down, she bent into joggers' pace against the wind, her feet picking up almost a sporting speed until she reached a hill. Then she climbed slowly and the gradient made itself felt. Straightening her back, she looked up momentarily to gauge the distance to the summit but found her view blocked by a man moving a few steps in front of her. He was bent almost double and was carrying a heavy load.

"Keep going," he called back to her, "keep going." In the mist she could discern only an outline of his figure. But she wondered how he could speak at all with what appeared to be a great weight on his back. The wind grew stronger and she became breathless. No matter how hard she tried she could not overtake the figure above her on the hill.

Perhaps, she thought, if I offered to help him shoulder that load we could make better progress together.

"Excuse me, Sir," she called, gasping for breath, "can I help you carry that?"

"When you can take it, you shall have it. It's yours," came the reply.

"But I'm just behind you, please let me carry it with you," she continued.

"It's yours," he said, without stopping or turning around. He kept walking. She felt slightly frustrated at his strange behavior and the fact that he was still in front, blocking her progress. Perhaps she ought to take the initiative. With an extra surge of energy she veered to the left, intending to sprint forward and overtake him. Immediately she felt the full force of the gale blowing down the mountain, forcing her backward. His body had been shielding her from its worst effects and she flung her arms out and caught his shoulders to save herself from being flung to the bottom of the hill again. As she did so she grasped the sturdy object of wood which he carried. It was a cross and written upon it was her name.

"It's yours," he repeated and with one arm steadied the cross and with the other cupped her shoulders, preventing her from being hurled back down the mountain. Together, they climbed.

Within the prayer healing ministry for more than twenty years now, I have heard a great deal of misguided pain expressed about "crosses." Not the one Jesus died upon, but the ones we are each told to shoulder on our journey through life. I believe that "the cross" we must carry is not an illness, a disability, an obnoxious relative, a lifetime's failure, or any other kind of misfortune that may befall us along the way. These are merely the barnacles which cling to us as we each sail on our journey through a broken and fallen world.

In our passage, Mark is speaking about the cost of discipleship: the cross that Peter had not realized he had dropped until the cock crowed three times; the cross that led Stephen to a stoning, that cost John the Baptist his head. It is the faithful, persistent, and consistent witness to the lordship of Jesus Christ, and our refusal to deny Jesus first place in our lives whatever the price, that is our cross.

Our traveler was enabled to carry hers by pacing one step behind the Savior and not attempting to overtake him. The great news is that the weight of it is not on our shoulders, but on his.

> *Dear Savior, there is no progress in my life*
> *worth the loss of your kingdom.*
> *Save me, not only from sin but also from*
> *my many daily attempts to run ahead of your will.*
> *Thank you for never doing anything for me that I can do for myself.*
> *Thank you also for walking on the steep places of my journey,*
> *bearing the weight of my cross on your shoulders.*
> *Forgive me if ever I deny that the steep climbs*
> *were your victories, not mine. Amen.*

P.S. God—About those small frustrations
that seem like crosses and really frustrate progress.
Thank you that they can be turned from negatives into positives.
Please show me how, in Jesus' name.

Week 3: Thursday
RISKING BEAUTY
Isaiah 52:7–10

> *How beautiful upon the mountains*
> * are the feet of the messenger who announces peace . . .*
> *who announces salvation,*
> * who says to Zion, "Your God reigns."*
> *Listen! Your sentinels lift up their voices,*
> * together they sing for joy;*
> *for in plain sight they see*
> * the return of the LORD to Zion.*
> *Break forth together into singing,*
> * you ruins of Jerusalem;*
> *for the LORD has comforted his people,*
> * he has redeemed Jerusalem.*
> *The LORD has bared his holy arm*
> * before the eyes of all the nations;*
> *and all the ends of the earth shall see*
> * the salvation of our God.*

Entering into the visual imagery of the passage, picture in your mind's eye a city, a huge city, and beyond it a mountain. The

73

people are huddled and harassed, walking its dark streets in fear, believing that mere survival is a prize worthy of the gargantuan struggle to make it through to the next day. A people in exile, hoping fervently that the wait will not be for much longer. The despair that hangs over the streets will lift, will dissolve like snow as the dawn warms its flakes to rain, when light comes.

Watchmen strain their eyes toward the hills for a sign, a glimpse of the long-expected messenger. Is he coming today? Will it be today? Then, slowly, walking on the mountain slopes, they see a man. At first they doubt their own eyes but as he approaches the gates of the city they see his face, shining with joy. His voice cries out the news, peace is possible, and hope. The nation is saved, the people can live.

From every house and basement the citizens run to meet him, falling down to kiss his feet with joy. They are callused feet and hard. The dried blood and blisters ugly from the arduous journey. A woman cups them in her hands and begins to sing, "How beautiful upon the mountains are the feet of the messenger who brings good news," and the poignancy and irony of the sentiment bring tears of joy and gratitude to every watcher upon the walls.

The traveler had rested in this waiting town for a short time, hoping that the messenger would come. She had sung the people's songs with them, had embraced their patience, had thrilled to their faithful worship. But it was Advent, and she must journey on, now that the messenger had come. Already the angel choirs were massing and if she was to know the peace that passes all understanding, the traveler would have to discover for herself who was visiting earth to dwell with humankind and bring peace.

In my pastoral work more seekers have agonized over the longing for peace than anything else in the Christian life. They

have sought it like an ointment to salve a bleeding heart; to oblit-
erate a feeling of guilt; to escape from an experience of stress.
Thank the Lord he also wishes to heal hearts, cleanse guilt, relieve
stress, but God rarely prescribes peace as the solution. For peace
is the aftermath, not the remedy. It comes only when the Lord
returns to Zion—that "Zion" being the most inner sanctuary of
our lives. It is the place where we stand naked before the Lord,
unworthy, yet unafraid, and only we can open the door and invite
God in.

Peace is not a serenity, a hiding place, a relief from trouble,
but it is attained by those messengers of God who are willing to
bring it to pass by walking barefoot across the jagged rocks of life,
tramping through mountain crevices of pain and suffering, of
betrayal and disappointment, and still to keep walking and, in
Christ's strength, see the journey through.

Yahweh, once this was a song of rejoicing
for ceremonial entry of the monarch toward enthronement.
Now I feel your people in their exile, longing for restoration.
Like them, we pray for freedom and hope.
In our exile from perfection, from sinlessness,
from full union with you,
we ask you, Lord, to make our ugliness of spirit clean and beautiful.
Make us like feet, mud-splattered by the journey,
yet made beautiful by the message of hope
and light that they bring. Amen.

Week 3: Friday
RISKING SATISFACTION
Isaiah 55:1–3

> *Ho, everyone who thirsts, come to the waters;*
> *and you that have no money, come, buy and eat!*
> *Come, buy wine and milk without money*
> *and without price.*
> *Why do you spend your money for that which is not bread,*
> *and your labor for that which does not satisfy?*
> *Listen carefully to me, and eat what is good,*
> *and delight yourselves in rich food.*
> *Incline your ear, and come to me;*
> *listen, so that you may live.*
> *I will make with you an everlasting covenant,*
> *my steadfast, sure love for David.*

Thank you, Isaiah, for your wonderful invitation to enjoy life and be satisfied. In previous chapters you outlined a vision for the people—a vision of salvation and promise, of humiliation and suffering. And you followed it up with the joyful goodness of an almighty God's invitation to receive and enjoy the bounty of his provision for all our needs.

Our traveler left behind a modern environment of financial constraints and material demands, where computer technology, credit cards and lottery tickets are offered by the media and society, cheek by jowl with carols, worship and nativity plays—all presented as legitimate accessories to the run-down to Christmas.

Our traveler stood gazing in a storefront on her journey, needing food and refreshment along the way. Her memory was filled with echoes from previous years of frantic Christmas shopping. Voices of children demanding the latest state-of-the-art gizmo, friends insisting, "Don't go to any trouble, now" and that last-minute rush to find a gift to satisfy that one person who has everything and for whom it is so difficult to buy.

"What do you buy for the person who has everything?" she heard herself asking aloud. Then the thought struck her forcibly that God is that very person. She was making a journey toward Jesus' birth, and without a gift in her hand. But there was nothing she could bring except herself.

The shop into which she stared was a bakery. The smell of freshly baked bread wafted out. She went inside and bought sandwiches for her own journey, and a cold drink to fill her thermos. It was a wonderful reassurance to imagine the living God taking pleasure in her enjoyment of God's bounty. How good the liquid would taste in this dry, parched land, how satisfying the sandwiches would be, she thought. How simple such a snack always seemed at home, yet here on a long journey with different priorities and God as the object of the quest, how she looked forward to the eating, with real anticipation. What had changed? she wondered. Certainly not the food and drink. It was she who was changing. She had chosen to journey toward God's destination. To God's invitation, "Come," she had stepped out along the way, and already the sights and sounds were smelling, tasting, feeling new, even those which would once have seemed mundane and commonplace.

Maybe it was her attitude that was altered. Perhaps she was attempting for God what once she had asked God to do for her, to satisfy.

"Come to the waters," God invites his people. The Lord could easily assuage our thirst by carrying the pitcher to our lips but instead invites, "Come." The journey is a large part of the satisfaction. Our engagement with a living God is, to the creator, vital, and should surely be, to us, more urgent than any need to match the destination with our flawed and petty sense of anticipation. Anticipate nothing, expect more than could ever be imagined. Risk the journey and see where creator and created will go together. The thirst is the thing, come and feel your thirst begin to be changed into something else until the goal is reached. Water, pure water, will surprise, will refresh, will renew, if the traveler refuses to be trapped by his own expectations. Step out, a well waits for you with water only God can give. But be prepared, it may be satisfaction of a nature never experienced before.

Isaiah, in recalling the people to the right priorities, acknowledging their human need for fulfillment and pointing them to the roots of satisfaction, shows that such satisfaction is everlasting, it is steadfast, and it is relational—the relationship between a living God and God's human creation. There is hope for us all when he cites the covenant entered into by God with David whom God loved. Yes, the same David who also failed God, the same David whose life was often lived "on the run," and what was God's response? Love, unconditional, unadulterated love. Now there's satisfaction!

Lord, your chosen people never did have an easy life,
not then, not in the 1940s, not now.

Show me what I need.
Then I'll know what to ask for to God's satisfaction. Amen.

Week 3: Saturday
RISKING ENCOUNTER
Malachi 3:1–4

See, I am sending my messenger to prepare the way before me, and the Lord whom you seek will suddenly come to his temple. The messenger of the covenant in whom you delight—indeed, he is coming, says the LORD of hosts. But who can endure the day of his coming, and who can stand when he appears?

For he is like a refiner's fire and like fullers' soap; he will sit as a refiner and purifier of silver, and he will purify the descendants of Levi and refine them like gold and silver, until they present offerings to the LORD in righteousness. Then the offering of Judah and Jerusalem will be pleasing to the LORD as in the days of old and as in former years.

Stepping out on the journey, the traveler risks encounter with a living God. Stables may hold lovable babies and thoughts of seasonal greetings and promises of light and the childhood memories of Santa Claus and turkey and cozy celebrations. But a journey to Bethlehem this year is not about decorating Christmas trees, it requires stepping toward the fire, prepared to surrender to the cleansing touch of rebirth.

The Bible's promise of the coming one in Malachi pulls no punches. An encounter with him is neither bland nor superficial.

He brings to the world a new order, prepares for a new kingdom, and will not share a place in our hearts with sin. Something has to go when we come face-to-face with a master whose nature is love and holiness and who cannot look on sin.

We must not walk toward Bethlehem with the ambition of cuddling the baby. The infant may be small but the shadow of the cross already falls across the manger. If this is to be our destination we must fear nothing, not even the refiner's fire.

The traveler stopped by the roadside for a rest and took out a sketchbook to doodle a picture of the imagined stable. She thought of all the nativity plays she had ever seen, the many Christmas cards bought and received through the years, the carols sung. Candles and tinsel, and a warm glow spilling from the extra efforts toward goodwill throughout society at this time of year. Soup distributed to the homeless people on the streets, smiles and season's greetings and a new start in the new year, all combine to conjure up a feeling of safety and comfort. How many folk think of Christmas as a children's time? she wondered. An idealistic holiday period of giving and receiving gifts, of love and family values despite the threats from an ever more secular world beyond the security of the Christmas tree in the living room? This year she was determined to see the real stable, to find the real child, and to kneel a little closer to the fold. Why should Christmas be either a madcap merry-go-round of frantic activity and pressurized preparations or, alternatively, an interlude of pleasantness in twelve months of mayhem?

When Malachi prophesied the coming redeemer he spoke of a new world order. A life changer who would be the light of the world—not a candle, or a dim lamp, but a fire. Darkness would not be reduced by the redeemer's presence, but obliterated. When a candle is brought into a room there is light, but there is also shadow. When Christ's fire enters a heart all else but light must be purged from it. There should be a warning sign hanging over the manger: "Dynamite. Handle at your own risk."

Our world, perhaps more in the West than elsewhere, is in danger of losing the sensation of respect and wonder and awe as we approach the stable. We often approach Calvary with mixed feelings and stand at a respectable distance, careful, for safety's sake. But during Advent we are tempted by the well-established routine and tradition both in church and society, to stroll to the stable unaware of the life-changing dynamic kicking his feet innocently in a feeding trough.

The traveler put away her sketchbook. She could not finish the picture until she had journeyed to Bethlehem. Not until she had encountered the child.

Dear God, no longer do I pray,
"What shall I do for a happy Christmas?"
I pray only, "How can I come close enough to your fire
to let it change me, to enable me to bring hope at Advent
to all those who walk with me on the journey of life?" Amen.

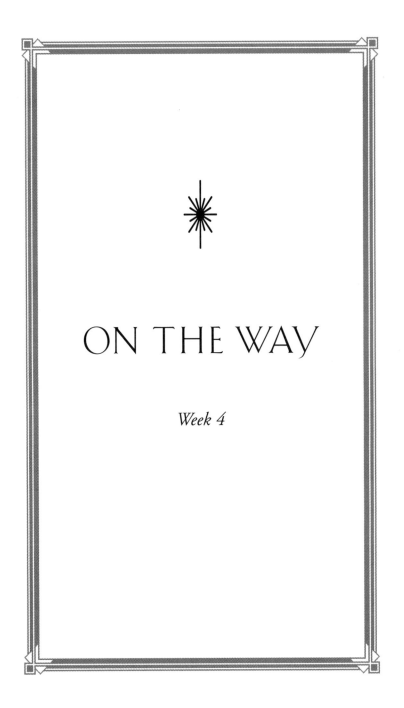

ON THE WAY

Week 4

Week 4: Sunday
THE INNKEEPER
Luke 2:1–7

In those days a decree went out from Emperor Augustus that all the world should be registered. This was the first registration and was taken while Quirinius was governor of Syria. All went to their own towns to be registered. Joseph also went from the town of Nazareth in Galilee to Judea, to the city of David. . . . He went to be registered with Mary, to whom he was engaged and who was expecting a child. While they were there, the time came for her to deliver her child. And she gave birth to her firstborn son and wrapped him in bands of cloth, and laid him in a manger, because there was no place for them in the inn.

The man came toward her at a brisk walk. She, on the other hand, was moving slowly along the rough path. She was tired. The exertion of leaving home and the luggage she still carried lay heavy upon her back.

"Excuse me, Sir," she called as he passed her, "is this the way to Bethlehem?"

"Yes, straight ahead," he called, "you'll see the signs."

"Where are you going?" she shouted.

"For provisions," he replied, retracing his steps to her side.

"I carry my food with me," she said, making herself comfortable on a nearby rock. "Would you like to have a share of my lunch?"

He hesitated and then, as she pulled sandwiches and drink from her luggage, he squatted beside the rock and scrutinized her face.

"You travel prepared," he said. "Not everyone thinks ahead."

There was something in the way he gazed into space that made her imagine there was a story in his throwaway remark.

"Are you thinking of anyone in particular?" she asked.

He smiled and then began the tale as they ate.

"A young couple came to my place looking for help once."

"Vagrants?" she queried.

"Oh, no," he laughed, "anything but! These were decent people, everything about them told me so. They were in town for the census. You remember the time when Augustus started numbering the people? The mother was expectant, otherwise I'd have sent them packing. Full up I was, I couldn't have squeezed as much as a mouse into the inn. Mary was the name of the girl. It looked like she was ready to give birth at any moment. I let them bed down in my stable. It was all I had left but they were very grateful. It was pretty rowdy in the inn that night, most of my guests turned their journey into an excuse for a celebration. Music, dancing, a whale of a time. The stable was probably the best chance of privacy I could afford the couple, rough though it was. Every so often I went to have a look at the animals and to see how the girl was getting on. My wife had set her up with clean water and blankets. Everything seemed to be in hand. I didn't even realize the baby had arrived until the people started coming."

"More guests?"

"No, people to see the newborn. I didn't know then how they'd heard but we were inundated with shepherds and locals. At the time I imagined that the word had spread by way of the traveling musicians who were performing from inn to inn. But what amazed me was the three astronomers from far out East who arrived in the town not long after, asking to see the child. Now, no grapevine works that quickly. Besides, they claimed they had known for ages that he'd be here. I had to live my whole life before I heard the complete story."

"You did the new family a great kindness," she commented.

"Kindness?" he smiled. "They did me a greater one."

Her puzzled expression encouraged him to continue.

"They used my shelter," he replied. He rose to his feet to journey on. "But you're headed for Bethlehem, aren't you? Keep on in that direction and you'll find out for yourself."

She called after him, "What happened to you?" But he was already around a bend in the road and she never did discover what path the innkeeper had taken on his journey.

Dear God, shelter me in your provision.
Forgive my constant obsession for fulfillment of my needs.
Rest me in the knowledge that you provide my resting place,
and more, much more. Amen.

P.S. God—If you'd stayed at my house, Lord,
it would have changed me,
I would have recognized you.
Or would I?
Please Lord, make it so, in Jesus' name.

Week 4: Monday
THE SHEPHERDS
Luke 2:8–14

*In that region there were shepherds living in the fields, keeping watch
over their flock by night. Then an angel of the Lord stood before them,
and the glory of the Lord shone around them, and they were terrified.
But the angel said to them, "Do not be afraid; for see—I am bringing you good news of great joy for all the people: to you is born this day
in the city of David a Savior, who is the Messiah, the Lord. This will
be a sign for you: you will find a child wrapped in bands of cloth and
lying in a manger." And suddenly there was with the angel a multi-
tude of the heavenly host, praising God and saying,*

> "Glory to God in the highest heaven,
>   and on earth peace among those whom he favors!"

After lunch she traveled on, determined to find one of those shepherds the innkeeper had spoken about. How did they know to
come to the stable? Was it the local gossip—or something more?

Asking in a village street, she got directions to a nearby field.
There she found an old man teaching his grandson how to tend
a sheep pen. It was nothing like the modern folds she had seen in
farms at home. Watching quietly in the background she listened
to the boy being instructed in the dubious art of sleeping across
the gap in the pen which was the entrance to the fold.

No door, she thought, no gate?

"Granddad," the child said, "what if a wolf comes, or a wild cat?"

"It must pass you first, child, before it gets a sheep."

The boy's eyes opened wide in fear. "But Granddad, it might eat me, and then the sheep."

The old man's face remained serious. "It might," he said, "so you'd better make sure it doesn't get through the gap, eh?"

At the woeful look on the child's face, the old man whispered gently, "That's what it means to be a shepherd, son."

She stepped toward the pair of them, now both deep in thought. "So it's a dangerous occupation, sheep-keeping?" she said to the old man.

"Not as terrifying as the night I first met the eternal shepherd," he replied.

"Tell me," she said.

He fixed his gaze on the distant hills and began, "How would you like to be sitting, sleepless, on a dark hillside for half the night struggling to keep your eyes open? Your body is numbed with the cold and lack of sleep, your brain too, yet you know that you are the only thing standing between your sheep and attack, perhaps even death. Suddenly the silence is shattered with deafening noise and a light so blinding you can't even see the animals anymore."

"I'd be scared," she said.

"Scared?" He grimaced. "I was terrified and the other men too. We didn't wait until morning. Ran the whole way down to Bethlehem. Took the sheep with us. We had to see if it was true. If he'd really come, if the prophecy had been fulfilled." Then, aside to the boy, "Don't you go trailing your livelihood after you in the night, boy, it does the sheep no good."

"But Granddad, you. . . ."

"Yes, yes, I know I did, but a thing like this doesn't happen twice in a lifetime—God bringing the choir to give you a message."

"And in the stable?" she prompted.

"Just a baby and his parents. The animals got a drink, though. For that we were grateful."

"Were you disappointed?"

"Well, the angels said he was the one. So we just had to have faith, didn't we? Years afterward we heard what happened to him. Terrible it was, an awful death. But it was then we knew it was true. He called himself the shepherd, that baby, when he'd grown. A shepherd doesn't stop at anything to save his sheep. We know. Yes, it was him all right. We were right to believe. No, we haven't been disappointed."

> Shepherd, you did that for me.
> Stretched full length in the gap.
> Took the full brunt of the savage attacks that I deserve,
> took them in my place.
> I journey in search of happiness.
> I chase after shelter and food and life while you seek only me.
> Savior, forgive, lead me to your side, no matter where you stand.
> Yes, Lord, even if it is in that threatening place,
> that gap where I am most vulnerable. Amen.

> P.S. God—I'm not sure which I should fear the most,
> the wild animals, or the angel choir.
> The animals have big teeth and claws
> but the message of glad tidings can tear your presuppositions
> and plans for the future into as many shreds.
> No wonder the angels began with "Do not be afraid."
> Help me approach Christmas with joy, in Jesus' name.

Week 4: Tuesday
THE WISE MEN
Matthew 2:1–6

*In the time of King Herod, after Jesus was born in Bethlehem of
Judea, wise men from the East came to Jerusalem, asking, "Where
is the child who has been born king of the Jews? For we observed
his star at its rising, and have come to pay him homage." When
King Herod heard this, he was frightened, and all Jerusalem with
him; and calling together all the chief priests and scribes of the
people, he inquired of them where the Messiah was to be born.
They told him, "In Bethlehem of Judea; for so it has been written
by the prophet:*

> *'And you, Bethlehem, in the land of Judah,
>   are by no means least among the rulers of Judah;
> for from you shall come a ruler
>   who is to shepherd my people Israel.'"*

It was nightfall when the camels came into sight against the outline of the sand dunes silhouetted against the night sky by a full
moon. No small rodents scampered before the soft pads of the
animals' feet, none risked the bright orb except the travelers. They
moved slowly but with purpose toward the oasis. She watched the
three men dismount and water their camels. There was an easy
grace about them, their deportment showing a dignity which
matched their elegant clothing.

The leader extended an arm in her direction and waved to
her politely.

"Madam, you require water?" he asked.

"Thank you, no," she said, "but I would value conversation."

They sat together, all four, around a small fire below palms that were more audible than visible despite the moonlight. The rustle of their long branches in the breeze gave her a sense of an unseen presence punctuating the storytelling.

In the semidarkness the tone of their words seemed almost conspiratorial except for the note of worshipful awe interjected at intervals as the men spoke.

They talked of stars and space and things to come. Of science and telescopes and whether one day humankind would travel to the outer ends of the galaxy. They spoke of vision and hope and one particular appearance in the sky of a star long foretold, linked as it was to God's own visitation of the planet earth, and how they knew God would come. How they'd followed the star to find God.

They had found first the wrong king, a tyrant, who had defrauded and murdered to enhance his power on earth, but God had guided them in a dream to avoid going near that monster again, showing them a safe way home.

"But in between," she said, "what did you find before going home?"

The wise man looked at her. "We found more than we could ever have imagined. A star fallen to earth in the shape of a little child, his mother Mary welcoming us in mingled puzzlement and joy, his father Joseph accepting our gifts of gold, frankincense and myrrh as he had previously welcomed the treasure of humble shepherds.

"Mary held the frankincense and myrrh a long time in her hands and we saw that she was quietly crying."

"Why do you think they made her cry?" the girl asked.

"Oh, I suppose they brought back memories of sorrowful

times and reminded her of the smell of death in funerals when they were burned as incense and used as preparation for burial."

"Why did you bring such gifts?"

Another of the wise men reached his hand to the ground at his feet. Scooping some sand with the tips of his fingers he held it up toward the fire. In the light of the dying embers the grains on his skin glistened.

"When a God makes himself so small that he is able to squeeze into a size no bigger than a tiny grain of sand or a human seed that makes a human baby, then a wise man knows that God will not scorn even death to secure life for all in human form, no matter how much lower and more base such a form might be compared to God's great glory. If God had become a baby he would not shirk from dying a human death."

"But we had to move fast to make our escape," said the leader.

"And have you escaped?" asked the girl.

"Yes, daughter," said the leader, "but will you?"

Savior, let me come to the manger willing to be reborn.
Lead me to the cross, willing to die.
Send me forward in your footsteps unafraid
because you have been here before me and illuminated the way.
This Christmas, select for me a brief moment
when I can creep beyond my home and stand
alone and silent below the stars.
Somewhere where no city lights dim their brilliance
or town buildings hide their canopy.
Let me gasp at the enormity of your cosmos,
thrill to the beauty of your creative thought, kneel in fresh
awareness of my own smallness

and feel again the call experienced by the wise men.
To journey, to risk, to seek and to embrace fully
life and life more abundant,
won for me at such a cost to you. Amen.

P.S. God—Scientists and shepherds,
all kneeling on straw to meet a baby king.
Thanks for the created elements that led the scientists,
and the visionary revelation that led the shepherds,
so that both those who follow head and those who follow heart
combine together to lead the world in unity
to your throne, in Jesus' name.

Week 4: Wednesday
A KING?
Matthew 2:7–12

Then Herod secretly called for the wise men and learned from them the exact time when the star had appeared. Then he sent them to Bethlehem, saying, "Go and search diligently for the child; and when you have found him, bring me word so that I may also go and pay him homage." When they had heard the king, they set out; and there, ahead of them, went the star that they had seen at its rising, until it stopped over the place where the child was. When they saw that the star had stopped, they were overwhelmed with joy. On entering the house, they saw the child with Mary his mother; and they knelt down and paid him homage. Then, opening their treasure chests, they offered him gifts of gold, frankincense, and myrrh. And having been warned in a dream not to return to Herod, they left for their own country by another road.

She stood before Herod, uncertain. She did not know why she had come to the palace. Perhaps to look the monster in the face. Maybe she thought his side of the story would prove the man not quite as evil as history had judged. Or she might have imagined she could reason with him, talk him out of his intentions, maybe even attempt to help save Herod's soul.

As he glared at her with cold hatred, more terrifying than burning anger, she realized she should not have come. The memory of slaughtered armies—and slaughtered children—shone, steel bright, from his eyes.

"I am king," he sneered.

"Whom do you fear?" she asked, her eyes leveled at his own, her palms damp.

"I fear no one," he said without hostility, stating it as a matter of fact.

"What right have you to rule?" she asked.

"I am king," he repeated without emotion.

"Show me a king's wisdom and understanding," she demanded, praying silently as she spoke.

His eyes and neck betrayed the calm tone of his voice as he rose to his feet. "Speak to my counselors on any subject," he said. "They have all wisdom and all knowledge and they are mine."

"Whom do you serve?" she asked.

"I am king," he roared. "All serve me."

She could see the unsatisfied lust for power in his eyes, the arrogance born of worldly strength and might. There was no soul-searching in this man. All he served stood reflected in his mirror.

"Come with me to Bethlehem," she invited. "Come alone, without advisors, or soldiers, or entourage. Please, just come see a palace without jewels or crowns. A king whose throne is a manger, whose power is love."

At the mention of "king" he advanced down the steps toward her with menace, his hand raised to strike. But the object of his rage was not herself. His hand fell upon the book held by one of his own advisors. It was the Book of Isaiah the prophet and in it was written why the Christ child would be king. Because the child's pedigree was as God had ordained, because God's spirit would rest upon him, because the wisdom and understanding and counsel and might would come from no spin doctors, nor man's arrogance but from God alone. If anything concerned the prince of peace it would be to obey God in heaven, even to the cross. The entire ambition and ethos of the promised one would be to work the will of God (Isaiah 11).

God, thank you for the wonderful experiences
given to the wise men
and for their deliverance when told to go home by another way.
I cannot change history, nor am I immune
to the consequences of other people's evil plans.
Please, God, grant that my actions are motivated by love
and my desires purified to ensure that no evil design
may recruit me to its will.
I want only to be the child of the prince of peace. Amen.

Week 4: Thursday
THE PROMISED ONE
Isaiah 11:1–3 (Read verses 1–9)

> *A shoot shall come out from the stump of Jesse,*
>   *and a branch shall grow out of his roots.*
> *The spirit of the LORD shall rest on him,*
>   *the spirit of wisdom and understanding,*
>   *the spirit of counsel and might,*
>   *the spirit of knowledge and the fear of the LORD.*
> *His delight shall be in the fear of the LORD.*

Here was real understanding and wisdom and counsel and might. Real pedigree and heritage and the Lord's favor. For a king? No, for one like a lamb to the slaughter. Sacrificed, not for power or prestige or wealth, but for the love of a race of humans on a tiny planet in a huge universe. A planet where lions and lambs normally eat each other and the snake's bite can be poisonous unto death.

The bite that beguiled Eve into disobedience against God. The bite that coerced Adam into disobedience against the same God. A bite that poisoned the entire human race forever.

Without this wonderful picture in Isaiah we might approach Christmas with as little hope as our traveler could realize standing before an unrepentant Herod. But the promise in Isaiah is of an upside-down world. A planet where everything is reversed from the evil and degradation of sin and shame back to its original purity and peace. Where even pain and suffering take on a new meaning and are robbed of their power to destroy just as death is robbed of its sting. Maybe we should say it is really a picture of the world turned "right side up" again.

The rest of the passage tells of savage beasts sharing the same shelter, innocent children recognized as more powerful than the worst evil. No more hurting nor destruction because the Lord's presence will then fill the whole earth so full that there will be no more room for anything but vintage love. "A little child shall lead them."

But not merely any child. The transformation of nature and creation is possible only as a result of the coming of a righteous king, a descendant of Jesse and continuing in King David's line. A ruler who will exhibit God's spirit in life and reign.

At the time of the census each family had to return to the city of their lineage and Joseph returned to Bethlehem, the city of David, because he was of the house of David (Luke 2:4).

To the people of Jesus' day, being able to trace your line in a family tree was very important, especially if it was to confirm eligibility, for the priestly class, for example. In the case of Jesus, both Matthew and Luke attempt to do so in terms of the priestly line and the royal heritage respectively. But both confirm the line from Jesse in accordance with Isaiah's prophecy.

Our traveler approached Bethlehem designing in her mind a suitable stable for a humble king. Perhaps it would be like those scenes in churches across her nation at Christmas, very small with lots of straw and carefully arranged figures facing front for the congregation to admire.

It would certainly have no luxury trappings of worldly royalty, just a clean, crisp, holy kind of aura, she imagined. She thought perhaps Joseph might welcome her and then usher her in quietly and introduce her to Mary before she was allowed to view the child. She did not expect to "fit in" exactly—after all, she belonged to a sophisticated era living in a new millennium, but she wouldn't let that prevent her from showing the proper respect. She hoped there would not be too many "locals" around as she wasn't sure how they might react to her company. Yes, she thought, it will be peaceful and brief, just long enough to show my respects and slip away again.

The town was bustling and noisy. The heat was almost unbearable. No one took the slightest notice of her as she stumbled to the inn. She found herself a number among countless others, all waiting to be numbered. If she had been a little less concerned with her safety, her need to find a bed for the night, her physical exhaustion, the important people she would soon meet in the stable, perhaps other questions might have sprung to her mind.

She might have taken time to ask herself, could people really change? Might the Monday morning feeling really not have to dominate the entire week? Can love be gentle and sacrificial and not abusive and harsh? Is an all-powerful creator prepared to walk in the slums of broken minds and broken hearts for no other reason than passionate, pure and sinless love? Could she ever see this creator, touch him? Could the creator really mend her broken heart? Was the journey worth the traveling? Had she arrived?

Dear Lord, there is a large hut up ahead, a simple stable.
Can I come in? Into the light?
Lord, is there room at the manger
for one more traveler tonight?

✳

For Christmas Eve and Christmas Day we have two readings which comprise a wholeness of approach to the central focus of this book. They can be read separately, but combined they provide a vehicle to assist the reader to enter into the experience of the first Christmas with new insight and by way of personal encounter.

You might like to take this approach:

Before reading:

* Pray and focus upon your own journey of life this far.
* Imagine how you might feel approaching the stable.
* Put aside all previous familiar or traditional visual images of the scene and ask God to bring a fresh experience of God's touch and a renewed sense of wonder and humility in his presence.
* Engage your heart as much as your head in these two readings.

After reading:

* "Feel" your surroundings—the smells, the sounds; sense the atmosphere.
* Open yourself to God in the silence.
* Praise God in thoughts of thanksgiving for where he has brought you in your own journey of life, then say in prayer what God prompts you to say.

You may wish to read both readings on Christmas Eve without a break and repeat this on Christmas Day to allow some time to bring you again to the subject with renewed vision. The second time through, you may wish to stop at intervals and imagine yourself speaking to each character in turn, the shepherds, Mary and Joseph and, most importantly, Jesus. Hear what they might have to say to you and then offer your conclusions to Jesus in prayer.

Christmas Eve
THE CHILD (I)
Isaiah 53:1–6

> *Who has believed what we have heard?*
> *And to whom has the arm of the LORD been revealed?*
> *For he grew up before him like a young plant,*
>   *and like a root out of dry ground;*
> *he had no form or majesty that we should look at him,*
>   *nothing in his appearance we should desire him.*
> *He was despised and rejected by others;*
>   *a man of suffering and acquainted with infirmity;*
> *and as one from whom others hide their faces*
>   *he was despised, and we held him of no account.*
> *Surely he has borne our infirmities*
>   *and carried our diseases;*
> *yet we accounted him stricken,*
>   *struck down by God, and afflicted.*
> *But he was wounded for our transgressions,*
>   *crushed for our iniquities;*
> *upon him was the punishment that made us whole,*
>   *and by his bruises we are healed.*
> *All we like sheep have gone astray;*
>   *we have all turned to our own way,*
> *and the LORD has laid on him*
>   *the iniquity of us all.*

It was the smell that hit her senses first. A mixture of cow dung and straw. She stooped slightly to move past the open wooden plank that served for a door into the stable. The oxen became uneasy at her presence. She felt out of her element, an alien, insecure. She pulled the hood of her new jacket over her head and hoped its designer label was sufficiently hidden.

She succeeded in shading the look of distaste on her face as she accidentally stepped in something inside that she most certainly felt should be outside.

In the middle distance, at a far corner of the animal stalls a single lamp spluttered a dim light, its wick almost burnt to extinction. At first, as she threaded herself awkwardly between the narrow stalls, she believed the shadows on the floor might be farm implements or other animals. Imagining that one of them had moved imperceptibly she approached cautiously, and discerned the outline of a man crouching with his back toward her, and then another and another. A small group in all, kneeling, crouching, squatting. No one standing but all remained still; they were perfectly still. One turned a face in her direction and she saw it was a woman's face. As it turned inward again, the traveler realized that she herself could not be seen by the people, although the animals seemed to sense her presence.

Like a fly on the wall she had arrived in the stable as an observer only. A traveler from another time, she had been granted the privilege of arriving without being there, of experiencing without touching.

A great sense of relief swept through her mind. She need fear no adverse reaction from the locals. She could learn and listen, and then escape home again. What was now clinging to the sole of her shoe would never have to be trodden into her luxury carpet. The stench in her nostrils would be gone forever when she wished it to be so. With a single thought she could banish all these disturbing sensations and images from her mind and be safe and secure once more in her familiar study at home, looking forward to a comfortable night's sleep in bed.

She turned toward the open entrance with one aim only, to flee into the fresh air and bright starlight beyond, when memories of the journey she had made began to flash before her mind.

The packing of the case. What an effort it had been to carry it this far. The rough road, the thirsty moments, the anticipation of great enterprise. The people met along the way, shepherds, kings, even the owner of this stable. What had he told her? "It was much later before I heard the complete story." She wanted to hear that story too. She had come this far. She owed it to herself to discover the truth.

Plunging her hand into her pocket she pulled out a handkerchief and smothered her nose and mouth in its scented depths as she turned again toward that quiet group in the shadows, bent in silent meditation.

There was a small space between two of the crouching figures and she squeezed through. Glancing at their faces, she recognized the shepherd she had met on her journey. One man there was a stranger to her and the woman also.

As she broke through the ring an object lay in front of her, stark and dilapidated, a manger. Its rough wooden edge caught her unawares as her elbow scraped against its corner, tearing the jacket. She let her luggage fall awkwardly to the dirty ground as, instinctively, she turned to inspect the torn material. It was the cry of a baby which halted her in midaction. . . .

Christmas Day
THE CHILD (II)
Isaiah 60:1–3

> *Arise, shine; for your light has come,*
>   *and the glory of the LORD has risen upon you.*
> *For darkness shall cover the earth,*
>   *and thick darkness the peoples;*
> *but the LORD will arise upon you,*
>   *and his glory will appear over you.*
> *Nations shall come to your light,*
>   *and kings to the brightness of your dawn.*

She bent over the lip of the dark makeshift cradle and peered, almost blindly, into an area hardly lit at all by the lamp. The child was swaddled tightly, the traditional bands of clothing allowing very little movement. The infant's head was swaying gently from side to side as if he was trying to see something. Then she realized, and the realization came as a terrible shock— he was trying to see her.

"You can see me?" she gasped, as if she expected an answer. Then she laughed, self-consciously and out loud, at her own stupidity. To have thought that a newborn infant could understand, never mind reply to, such a question!

Immediately the child laughed also. A gentle, warm sound of empathy and love. It reached out and lightened the dark surroundings. It touched her bent figure and spread its soft insistency back down the pathway of her journey, enlightening every memory, warming every cold step along the way. The truth held her captive and motionless. This child needed no skills of language or art of humankind to touch her at a level deeper than she had ever been touched before. This child could engage her soul.

Suddenly the room was full of mutterings, like a wave at full tide, the garbled whispers swelled to a crescendo and swept in upon her mind, threatening to swamp her with the culmination of its emotional trauma. She whirled around to face the semi-circle of crouched worshipers, expecting to see their faces animated in conversation. But all were still. Yet the noise grew in intensity and with the rise in volume it became less garbled and individual phrases and sentences became distinguishable within the tide of sound. She began to realize that what she was hearing were their thoughts. With telepathic clarity she focused on each in turn and was able, momentarily, to block out the remainder.

Concerns pushed from their minds to hers, the price of lambs, the need for good pasture, family illnesses, and memories, lots of memories. The shepherds' minds were full of singing. The flashback of a huge choir in the sky, not human but angelic. She heard the singing in their heads and could only gasp with wonder at the beauty of it. Like liquid sunlight against dark wet rockface, the room glistened with it. But the darkness seemed shattered by another light.

Pervasive and all-powerful, it came from somewhere in the depths of their worship. It was a sensation of great light, not blocking out their concerns, but enlightening every thought to brightness and banishing the darkness. It was the child.

He lay in the dark manger. But because he lay within that darkness, all was light.

She struggled to isolate one train of these telepathic mutterings from others and, as like is drawn to like, she focused upon the woman's thoughts. The same instant as she did so, a pain as sharp as any sword plunged into her side and she cried out in agony. The woman in her recognized that this was no pain of childbirth, but more, something much more. It traveled upward, upward, passing through her very heart till it flung itself beyond her body and mind and stood, in a reality that was stronger than virtual. It stood behind the silent people upon the stable floor. She recoiled from it in terror. The shadow had taken the shape of a cross.

The dying lamplight behind it etched its shape across the manger, pressing its blackness upon the baby's face. The infant did not cry, but struggled again to turn his head in her direction. The light in the child's eyes was not darkened by the shadow. The shadow was made translucent by the strength of love within the manger. For long moments she was held by that look. Time became meaningless as the two remained locked in perfect engagement. She had joined the worshipers. They were one in surrender, in light, with joy.

Savior, forgive.
Dear Lord, you came,
you died,
you rose.
I come. Amen.

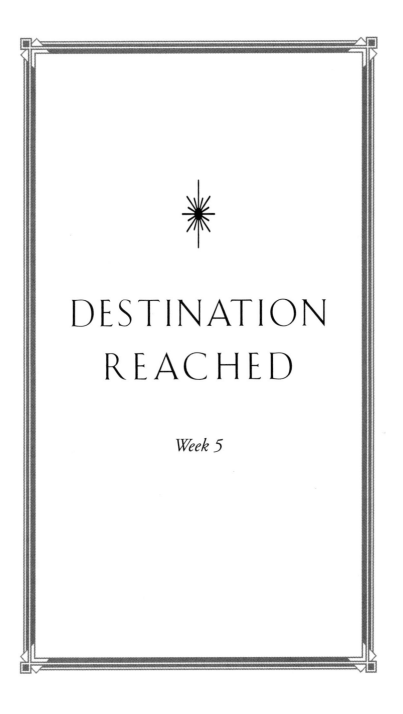

DESTINATION REACHED

Week 5

Week 5: Sunday
THE LIGHT
Isaiah 9:2–6

> *The people who walked in darkness*
> *have seen a great light;*
> *those who lived in a land of deep darkness—*
> *on them light has shined.*
> *You have multiplied the nation,*
> *you have increased its joy;*
> *they rejoice before you*
> *as with joy at the harvest,*
> *as people exult when dividing plunder.*
> *For the yoke of their burden,*
> *and the bar across their shoulders,*
> *the rod of their oppressor,*
> *you have broken as on the day of Midian.*
> *For all the boots of the tramping warriors*
> *and all the garments rolled in blood*
> *shall be burned as fuel for the fire.*
> *For a child has been born for us,*
> *a son given to us;*
> *authority rests upon his shoulders;*
> *and he is named*
> *Wonderful Counselor, Mighty God,*
> *Everlasting Father, Prince of Peace.*

Here is the light at last, the messianic hope of Israel who was to take his place in royal succession on the throne. In Bethlehem's stable we can affirm, as Christians, more than Isaiah knew. We can affirm that Yahweh's son is Jesus.

Our traveler walked from the stable not alone anymore, nor was she afraid. Jesus would deal with the fears in Jesus' time, in Jesus' way. She would no longer be driven by them but led by the Lord through the very midst of terror to safety. Darkness, she now knew, could take control only in the absence of light. The Savior had come, and now there would always be light. She could go home.

It was only when she reached the outskirts of the town on the far side of Bethlehem that she realized what was missing. Enthralled by the sensation of God's presence, she had not noticed what she had left behind. But now, fleet of step and moving in joy, her arms free and swinging loose by her side, she looked down and saw that her luggage was gone. She had left it where it had fallen upon the dirty ground beside the manger. She recalled last seeing it slumped at the foot of the shadow of the cross.

Instinctively she was tempted to retrieve it but instead she sat down on a nearby rock and contemplated its contents: all the provisions she packed for the journey, now half-eaten and much thrown away that had gone bad in the heat; the maps, the insurance, the extras—just in case. The worries, the bitterness, the unforgiveness, the grudges, the itinerary, the diary, the carefully worked out, itemized, cataloged agenda, the plans, the hopes, the anticipations, the fears, the "what ifs" and the "if onlys" and. . . . She was laughing now, really laughing. A childlike, unfettered, unmoderated, rolling-on-the-ground release of tension and anxiety and burden. At last she was free. Then, without glancing backward, she turned her face forward to go home, praying step-by-step.

Dear Lord, I acknowledge your sovereignty.
Please rule my life with love.
I recognize your wisdom.
Please grant me your guidance.
Knowing your mighty power, I pray for strength.
God, make me your child forever,
and teach me how to bring peace to those around me
as I become servant to the prince of peace. Amen.

Sun and Son
The way home
Turn on a light
Expels the darkness
That's what God did
when He had Jesus
come to earth as a baby;
to grow to manhood.

TO MEDITATE UPON THE NAMES
OF THE SAVIOR

Feel the wonder, refuse to let it die.
When wonder dies, we lose half the battle for life.
His name shall be called Wonderful.

Take his healing.
When we stop listening, our ears lose the ability to hear.
His name is Wonderful Counselor.

Kneel at his throne.
There is no greater power on earth than his.
His name is Mighty God.

Trust a perfect parent without human failings.
His name is Everlasting Father.

Peace flows from his soul to yours.
His name is Prince of Peace.

Week 5: Monday
THE INNOCENTS
Matthew 2:13–18

Now after they had left, an angel of the Lord appeared to Joseph in a dream and said, "Get up, take the child and his mother, and flee to Egypt, and remain there until I tell you; for Herod is about to search for the child, to destroy him." Then Joseph got up, took the child and his mother by night, and went to Egypt, and remained there until the death of Herod. This was to fulfill what had been spoken by the Lord through the prophet, "Out of Egypt I have called my son."

When Herod saw that he had been tricked by the wise men, he was infuriated, and he sent and killed all the children in and around Bethlehem who were two years old or under, according to the time that he had learned from the wise men. Then was fulfilled what had been spoken through the prophet Jeremiah:

> *"A voice was heard in Ramah,*
> *wailing and loud lamentation,*
> *Rachel weeping for her children;*
> *she refused to be consoled,*
> *because they are no more."*

No woolly lambs in this story. This is Christmas raw in tooth and claw. A loving God allowing a murderer to win, or did he? In love God permits us all to have free will. No one is forced into God's will. God designs no evil nor forces good upon anyone. The alternative to this would be a planet of puppets, and the very ones who might protest strongly against injustice to the innocent might be the same folk who would protest more strongly if their own freedom to choose was removed.

We cannot have our cake and eat it too. We can't shake our finger at God and wish him to destroy the Herods of this world because they are, in our estimation, "evil," and yet say, "Hands off, God" if the Lord attempts to force us out of our impatience, intolerance or unforgiveness. It's easy to forget that these and many other character traits and behaviors are also evil in God's sight. If God were also to remove this evil then we would disappear from the face of the earth.

God is in control, and one day he will say to all things evil, including Satan, "Thus far and no further," but God is giving his created beings a chance to choose good or evil before taking this drastic action.

From a lifetime of living with the challenge of multiple congenital disabilities, I know that what we observe at face value is never the whole story. God never contradicts God's own nature, and that nature is love. As the Lord touched Jeremiah in the womb (Jeremiah 1:5), so the Lord touches all his children, not to send problems or suffering, but to transform the consequences of living on an imperfect planet which is broken by sin, to change negatives into positives—that's if we choose to let God do so.

Jeremiah's call was a lifetime's personal commitment to God and he acknowledges that the divine plan for his life was designed and established by God even before Jeremiah's birth. This impetus to fulfill a dynamic purpose within the will of God was the secret of Jeremiah's strength and determination, evident throughout his life and ministry. For myself also, such impetus has guided me through times of great struggle, difficulties and pain, and allowed me to hear God speak to my heart, saying, "Let's see what we can do with this together." It is not our circumstances which dictate our future, or the outcome of those circumstances, but rather whether we allow God mastery of our lives.

Did Herod win? The Christ child was protected—but not from the cross. God took the suffering at Calvary to bring us the gift of eternal life.

Our traveler on her journey home still hears the cries of the dying babies and the mothers weeping. The sounds mingle with God's agony on the cross. There is no victory without suffering, there is no salvation without sacrifice. There is no discipleship without cost.

I thank the Lord that Herod was not the victor and, as for the innocents, I know that I cannot imagine the full story. But, from my own life's experience of how God continually enters into my situation, not necessarily to change the circumstances, but always to transform the situation from within, then I know that there are a myriad untold stories from the Rachels and the children. I look forward to hearing these voices of witness to God's empowering grace when I finally go home to the Lord.

Dear God, it hurts, Lord, but not from you.
I weep, Lord, but you do not desert me in my pain.
Separation from your love—that would be worst of all.
Thank you, God, that such an agony
can never be when Christ is in control.
Thank you for grace to choose
to surrender all control to Jesus. Amen.

Week 5: Tuesday
SMALL *IS* GREATEST
Philippians 2:5–11

> *Let the same mind be in you that was in Christ Jesus,*
> *who, though he was in the form of God,*
> *did not regard equality with God*
> *as something to be exploited,*
> *but emptied himself,*
> *taking the form of a slave,*
> *being born in human likeness.*
> *And being found in human form,*
> *he humbled himself*
> *and became obedient to the point of death—*
> *even death on a cross.*
>
> *Therefore God also highly exalted him*
> *and gave him the name*
> *that is above every name,*
> *so that at the name of Jesus every knee should bend,*
> *in heaven and on earth and under the earth,*
> *and every tongue should confess*
> *that Jesus Christ is Lord, to the glory of God the Father.*

As the traveler walked onward, the images and lessons of the journey played through her mind like a continuous recording of sensation and stimulation. Her frustration at the difficulties on the road, her anger at Herod's intransigence and killing. Her exhaustion on the steep hills, her fascination listening to the kings, wonder at the shepherd's tale, the shabby poverty and joy of the stable encounter, and ultimate surrender to the Lord.

In what mind should she arrive home? Confident, successful, what? She remembered those days of struggle as she had prepared to leave home at the start of the journey, every motivation, all the fears and urges that drove her to search for the unknown. What would the people at home think of the one who had left heaven to risk earth? Tears were in her eyes as she remembered the baby's face, his gentle laughter, the touch of his gaze, the power of his presence.

How could Jesus have come? How could Jesus have brought himself to that? The one who created the universe, how could he squeeze himself so small to become no bigger than a tiny seed that makes a baby, that travels through a messy birth channel to be spilled on to a dirty, unhygienic stable floor? How could Jesus do that? Not to speak of Calvary, or pain, or betrayal, or the death process, or the journey to hell and back and still coming to take up residence in each human person who chooses to grant the Holy Spirit tenancy of his or her life.

What entity could empty himself so totally for the sake of beings so inferior to himself that they hardly register on the scale of "mind" at all in comparison?

She knelt in awe of such a person of pure holiness, totally obedient to his father in heaven. An intellect so completely in love with humanity that there is nothing he would not do to save that same humanity, even while it denies its own need to be saved. This mind, she realized, contained the same attitude which she needed to have on her arrival home. Jesus' priorities, Jesus' positive thoughts in the place of negatives, Jesus' encouragement to others in the place of criticism, gentle words replacing harsh ones, trusting confidence in place of questioning self-doubts, humility in the place of arrogance and pride.

She was crying now as she felt the full enormity of Jesus' sacrifice. As she tried to imagine how one so great could become so small and realized how much time and effort the inhabitants of earth invest in the struggle to become great in their own eyes.

Kneeling there, by the roadside, her prayer was for smallness. A seed of hope to plant Jesus' light and salvation in every heart she met.

> *Dear Lord, you are to me that great and holy name*
> *to whom I bow. You are raised above all the sleaze and grime*
> *of earth's petty grievances and demands,*
> *the king of kings in glory forever.*
> *But the route to your station at God's right hand*
> *took you through some pretty muddy experiences.*
> *Thank you for embracing the pain for me.*
> *Small is great, let me never forget it. Amen.*

> *P.S. God—Help the "big" people of this world*
> *to be unafraid to be vulnerable.*
> *Some are men, some women, some authorities,*
> *but all are power-seekers.* ~ Big People
> *It is in being vulnerable that we learn fully*
> *to lean completely upon you and discover that your strength*
> *is indeed made perfect in weakness.*

Week 5: Wednesday
THE PRICE
John 3:16–21

For God so loved the world that he gave his only Son, so that every-
one who believes in him may not perish but may have eternal life.
Indeed, God did not send the Son into the world to condemn
the world, but in order that the world might be saved through
him. Those who believe in him are not condemned; but those who
do not believe are condemned already, because they have not
believed in the name of the only Son of God. And this is the judg-
ment, that the light has come into the world, and people loved
darkness rather than light because their deeds were evil. For all
who do evil hate the light and do not come to the light, so that
their deeds may not be exposed. But those who do what is true
come to the light, so that it may be clearly seen that their deeds
have been done in God.

When I teach in a school, I sometimes bring a parachute. A tent
is made of it, using a teacher as the tent pole and the pupils as the
tent pegs, sitting on the inside, anchoring it down by tucking the
material behind their backs and under their bottoms. In the very
short time that it is safe to stay in there, before the air runs out, the
children often respond to this cozy and intimate space by curling
comfortably into little balls. One Christmas, working with a group
of slow learners, I asked one little boy in such a position, "How do
you feel?" His answer came with a big smile. "Small," he said, and
then, as he was told how Jesus had squeezed himself as small as a
human can be, to become a little baby, which was first a tiny seed,

the child's face showed such wonder and amazement as to bring home the reality of the incarnation fresh to me again. "Big God?" he shouted, incredulous, "the big, big God!" he repeated, springing to his feet and stretching his arms as if to describe the whole universe. We grow into adults and imagine we become sophisticated, but may the creator help us if we ever lose the wonder of what God actually did at Christmastime, to say nothing of Calvary!

A God who could relinquish all power and rights in order to enter earth's history and rescue us from our sin and despair by sacrificing his own life must love us dearly. If the traveler is to bring the "baby" home at Christmastime she must acknowledge that the Christ, grown up, crucified and risen, is none other than God's son. She must submit her life and will to the Savior entirely, and live, breathe and act from then on in the light of the Lord's teaching and love.

As our traveler's thoughts dwelled on all that God had become and all God had given up for her, it was like an opening up within her. Deep inside she felt a turning, a slow dawning of light. Like the snatch of an old familiar tune, or a scent evocative of a foundational memory from the past, she knew she stood on firm reality again and her heart rejoiced. The holy book, long perched on the top shelf of her kitchen cabinet at home, had lain shut and dust-covered for decades.

But now, a long distance from home, words from that book came back into her mind. The best-known verse in the Bible, "For God so loved the world that he gave. . . ." The wonder was that the price is paid, that God loves unconditionally and the fresh start which a new year affords can be a true beginning if Christ is accepted as master.

The traveler had journeyed far. She had come to the light. She had rejected the darkness. Now she realized that Bethlehem was not the destination but a signpost along the way. Beyond it lay the cross and the empty tomb and beyond that her whole life was a journey of learning how to follow the Savior, how to obey him, how to receive his love and to become love, through the Savior, for others. Suddenly the road seemed longer and "home" appeared in her mind as a temporary bed and breakfast. The traveling was infused with a sensation of journeying toward a new home, an eternal destination, an exciting entity, and the realization was joy itself.

She wanted to identify the center of her universe—to examine how her time was spent, how her money was allocated, what made her angry or frustrated. Is it, she thought, world injustice, persecution of the weak in society, lack of compassion in the church, is this what touches my emotions and motivates my actions? Or could it be little things like when criticism galls, or somebody does me a bad turn, or when a wrench falls into the works of a carefully planned day?

She remembered the times she had extolled the virtues of a physical fitness workout, or made a healthy diet resolution. Now she prayed for the courage to initiate a spiritual health check—a motivations examination asking, "To what end do I rise every morning, toil every day, feel justified lying down to sleep each night?" God's word assured her that Christ had come, not to condemn but to save. Nevertheless she challenged herself to have the integrity and courage to feel condemned by love, knowing that when God's unconditional love touches, then that which is not love can feel only shame.

Lord, could I be love for you?
Could others drink of me and have no more thirst?
Might my touch show them that
I have felt your touch in me and can now pass it on?
Could I . . . may I . . . please let me
bring the baby home. Amen.

Week 5: Thursday
GOOD NEWS
John 5:25–30

Very truly, I tell you, the hour is coming, and is now here, when the dead will hear the voice of the Son of God, and those who hear will live. For just as the Father has life in himself, so he has granted the Son also to have life in himself; and he has given him authority to execute judgment, because he is the Son of Man. Do not be astonished at this; for the hour is coming when all who are in their graves will hear his voice and will come out—those who have done good, to the resurrection of life, and those who have done evil, to the resurrection of condemnation.

As our traveler continued on her way, she saw an old man stumbling toward her. He glanced longingly at her rock seat before flinging himself and his heavy sack on the ground beside her. The sack tipped over and scattered his belongings on the ground.

His eyes were closed and she quietly moved to gather up his stuff without disturbing him. "Come, sit here," she whispered as she replaced the last of his things into the sack. He opened his eyes and, wheezing from the effort, permitted her to help him onto the rock.

"Have you far to go?" she asked him.

"It makes no difference," he panted, "I'll never make it!"

"Perhaps after a rest and refreshment," she said.

"No, I'm a dead man already."

"You still breathe, you walk," she said. "You can make it."

"How would you know?" he snapped. "It's a long way to Bethlehem, and I'm tired."

"I know you can make it," she replied, "because I've been there."

The old man raised his head and looked her squarely in the face. "You've been there?"

"Yes, I have, all the way to the stable."

His face became animated and he grasped her arm with the urgency of desperation.

"You found it?" he gasped. "You got inside?"

She nodded and his questions tumbled one after the other like a torrent.

"How did you find the way? Was the door guarded? Were you searched? Did they ask for identification? Had you to pay? How many were there? Was it dark inside? What did you find?"

She spoke quietly, "He was there."

A look of fear shadowed the man's face.

"The judge," he stuttered. "You saw the judge?"

"I saw the child," she said.

The man seemed to hear nothing of her reply but started to shake and his body convulsed in spasm as he released a verbal river of tortured phrases.

"He won't listen. He doesn't know what I've been through. How does he know? He can't understand. He doesn't know what it's like. Who does he think he is? How can I tell him? How can I make him understand? How can I make him? . . ."

His anguished cries had risen to a crescendo until his coughing interrupted his own tortured words of fear and anger. She took his frail shoulders in her arms and rocked him gently back and forward like a baby. "Listen," she said softly, "please listen to me." As he became calm with exhaustion she told him the good news. "Jesus is here," she said. "Jesus made the journey to earth to experience for himself your pain. Jesus knows what you've been through because Jesus has been to the same planet, has been through the same brokenness, experienced the worst it can do to a man. Jesus obeyed God and has rightly deserved the title of 'judge' and Jesus will judge one day. But long before that you can start again. No matter how bad it has been, you can start again. Experience how trustworthy Jesus is, how deeply Jesus cares, how sacrificially Jesus loves you."

She longed to remove the burden of fear from the man but she knew he would not be able to let the luggage go until he met the one whose love casts out all fear. So she could only help him back on to his feet and wave as he turned toward Bethlehem. She heard him mutter as he left, "No, no, it's too late for me."

"It's never too late," she whispered, "never too late for resurrection."

Dear Savior, judge me in your love, and in your mercy forgive.
Give me courage to expose my worst side to you
and release it into your hands for judgment,

and for remolding and for healing.
Help me choose life, not death, for the new year. Amen.

P.S. God—I saw a card in a shop and had to buy it.
It was the tomb of Lazarus and Jesus standing outside calling,
"Come out, Lazarus."
From inside a "thought balloon" bellowed out
the response from Lazarus.
It bore the legend, "But I look terrible!"

Week 5: Friday
SING A NEW SONG
1 John 4:18–21

There is no fear in love, but perfect love casts out fear; for fear has to do with punishment, and whoever fears has not reached perfection in love.

Psalm 96:1–6

O sing to the LORD a new song;
sing to the LORD, all the earth.
Sing to the LORD, bless his name;
tell of his salvation from day to day.
Declare his glory among the nations,
his marvelous works among all the peoples.
For great is the LORD, and greatly to be praised;
he is to be revered above all gods.
For all the gods of the peoples are idols,
but the LORD made the heavens.

Honor and majesty are before him;
strength and beauty are in his sanctuary.

Praise is at the very heart of worship. It was for the Jews and it is for the Christian. The Psalms are full of exhortation to sing. Singing enables us to magnify the Lord, heartens the spirit and bonds the unity of those who lift their voices together. No wonder God loves to hear us sing. What more joyful exercise could start a new year?

But what if you can't sing? When I was a child, every time I woke early I would take my hymnbook and disturb the rest of the family, piping my favorite hymns as loudly as I could. The trouble was, I couldn't sing. One aspect of my disability is that I hear on one side only and cannot really discern the proper tone or pitch of my own singing voice, despite the fact that I am able to appreciate and play music and indeed to teach it to others. It was not long before someone outside the family told me quite cruelly the truth of this and my early morning praises ended. Sadly, I have not been able to attempt this since, but I continue to believe and pray that, one day, I will discover a brave teacher who, like myself, believes in miracles and will find a way to help me remedy the situation. Although I miss singing very much and my life is somewhat impoverished by its absence, God has seen to it that I am given plenty of opportunities to praise the Lord in other ways and my speaking voice is rarely silent in this endeavor.

But what if a person cannot sing for other reasons? Sadness, or sorrow, or a cold bitter hardness of heart, or churlishness against God? Some cannot sing because they are bored with the old song. If any of these reasons prevents us from singing on this new year's day, we can learn to sing anew the old song of God's love and God will enable us to sing a new song of hope and joy and peace for the coming year. If things are bad, remember, they can change, they don't have to stay like this forever. God is working, even now, for your very best. Begin by meeting the Lord halfway. Start by singing God's praises, whether you feel like it or not. Let the Lord lift your spirits, and the rest will follow, in the Lord's time.

As our traveler resumed her own journey homeward she thought of those waiting for her, old friends, family, colleagues. Could she help them to sing anew the old song or share with them the joy of singing for the first time the new song of "good tidings of great joy"? Could she hold them, metaphorically, in her arms, as they released their anger and hurt and fear? How much of it would be directed at herself? In some cases it might even be well deserved. Could she cradle them whether their anger was justified or not? Would God's love in her be strong enough for that? "Begin this new year in love," God seemed to say to her, in love with God's will, and God's people.

A crossroads lay ahead, with a signpost to every destination including home. The decision is the same for each of us. Do we choose escape from the broken and hurting people of the world or embrace full responsibility to be a part of their healing? The way of the cross is to face our fears and return home to the very heart of the turmoil. The traveler remembered the baby's cry, the baby's laughter, the baby's touch, the shadow of the cross. She did not hesitate but walked straight ahead on her original course, and her voice rose singing in praise to the Savior as her steps continued homeward bound.

Dear Lord, put within my heart the hope of your promises.
I know you are faithful and have great plans for me.
Forgive me when I get stuck in boredom, or bitterness.

Prepare my mind and put a new song in my heart for the new year.
I know the words, please teach me the tune. Amen.

Week 5: Saturday
THE RESPONSE
John 3:1–6

Now there was a Pharisee named Nicodemus, a leader of the Jews.
He came to Jesus by night and said to him, "Rabbi, we know that
you are a teacher who has come from God; for no one can do these
signs that you do apart from the presence of God." Jesus answered
him, "Very truly, I tell you, no one can see the kingdom of God
without being born from above." Nicodemus said to him, "How
can anyone be born after having grown old? Can one enter a sec-
ond time into the mother's womb and be born?" Jesus answered,
"Very truly, I tell you, no one can enter the kingdom of God with-
out being born of water and Spirit. What is born of the flesh is
flesh, and what is born of the Spirit is spirit."

How shall I tell them? she wondered, as she journeyed on. Will they
believe me? How can I help them understand? How could she
explain an empowerment that owes nothing to human structures or
business strategies or professional agendas? How could she share an
enablement that needs no state-of-the-art technology or intellectual
prowess? How could she offer them an energy source invisible to the
naked eye, dependent upon no mineral, no electricity, no nuclear
fuel, a resource initiated by no power games, or manipulation, directed
only by selfless love? A source foreign to the planet yet by no means

ignorant of it? It would be like speaking a different language to a culture that once used that language as its native tongue but that had long since allowed it to depreciate and decay until there was left only the faintest residue of the words, now without meaning.

Could she find that residue once more? Whisper it closely to their ears till the haunting, healing wonder of its music resurrected a faint echo of a folk memory, lyrical but unintelligible, in the harsh, jangling, virtual reality of a modern freeze-dried world?

"Jesus," she prayed, "do I talk of doctrines and theology, speak of commandments and law, preach of mercy and truth? God, do I take them to the heart of nature and show them the beauty of your creation? Holy Spirit, do I? . . ."

But when she turned to speak with the Spirit, the Spirit was gone, blowing where he willed, free and unfettered, moving on ahead of her to encounter the very people for whom she prayed.

Then she heard the Savior's words, "No one can see the kingdom of God without being born from above."

Born, she thought, like a seed. A tiny thing as small as a mustard seed, as small as the beginnings of faith.

Born, she thought, like nine long months of waiting in the semidarkness, dependent on every rise and fall of the host body, feeding from its food, allowing waste to be removed by its disposal processes, not knowing, not seeing, not understanding what lies ahead, merely "being" in trust. A hanging free in a cocoon of total reliance for every need, a surrender to oneness, a surrender to the greater power, of unconditional love itself.

Born, she thought, cataclysmic labor pains thrusting through the body of host and child till all previous states of comfort and complacency are ripped away in a vast surge like the thrust of repentance as the soon-to-be newborn endures that pain for all the hope of a new life at the end of the birth channel.

Born, she thought, not in body or by fleshly desire, but feelings born to new heart, mind to new thinking, soul to the freedom of truth. The truth of the child who is God's son, the child who is master to those who choose to follow him.

God, I believe in your son, Jesus.
Jesus, save me from my sin.
I am unclean till you wash me.
Spirit, enter this poor material body in union with my spirit
and make me a dwelling for the living God.
Birth me now within your will. Amen.

MEDITATION

※

I saw a spiritual newborn today, Lord.

Kicking like a baby, red-faced and lungs expanded
to full stretch as it screamed in protest at the new sensation
of having to work for breath to live. Laid naked upon your
nail-pierced palms, it punched the air before its blind eyes
while you gently turned the corner of your pure white robe
to wipe its nostrils and unblock its ears.
I saw it roll its head with tiny whimpers of joy as it sensed
the cool breeze of your breath blowing softly across its brow,
until the pain left its body and the torment fled from its mind.
When the splash of water came, it convulsed in a glorious
spasm of shock and stimulation, eyes open wide to focus at last
upon your smiling face. When fire and water mixed
there was no dowsing of the flames.
Fire kissed but did not burn, the child was born.

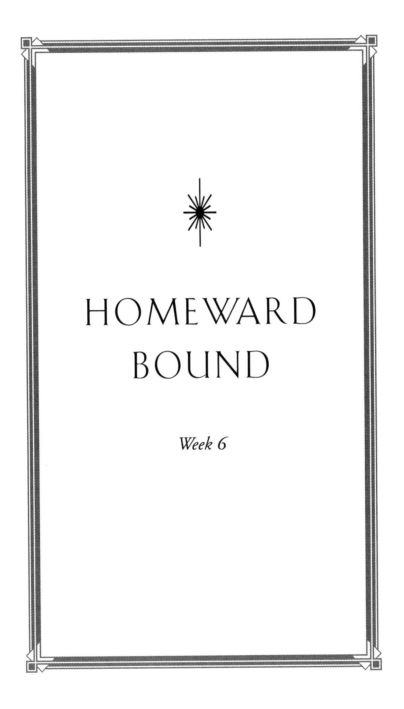

HOMEWARD
BOUND

Week 6

Week 6: Sunday
GOD WITH US
1 Kings 8:23–27

*O LORD, God of Israel, there is no God like you in heaven above
or on earth beneath, keeping covenant and steadfast love for your
servants who walk before you with all their heart, the covenant
that you kept for your servant my father David as you declared to
him; you promised with your mouth and have this day fulfilled
with your hand. Therefore, O LORD, God of Israel, keep for your
servant my father David that which you promised him, saying,
"There shall never fail you a successor before me to sit on the
throne of Israel, if only your children look to their way, to walk
before me as you have walked before me." Therefore, O God of
Israel, let your word be confirmed, which you promised to your
servant my father David.*

*But will God indeed dwell on the earth? Even heaven and the
highest heaven cannot contain you, much less this house that I
have built!*

"But will God indeed dwell on the earth?" asked King Solomon
as he dedicated his life's work, God's temple, built as a testimony
to the living God, the focal point of Israel's nation and worship.
The temple housed the ark of the covenant and, to a real extent,
represented to the people the place where God met the earth. It
was a building of sacrifice and redemption, a symbol of God's
promises and the responses of the chosen people to their creator-
savior. Yet Solomon's wonder and amazement still asked that
question, "God—dwell on earth?"

In spite of all that the Lord had done for Israel, despite their relationship through the ages, God still seemed too great to be touched, too mighty to be approached without sacrifice, too wonderful even to have God's name spoken. God's "otherness" had walked with them through the centuries, but "other" God was and the earth was a poor place to invite his visitation.

In Bethlehem's stable all that changed. God did not merely "visit" but broke irreversibly into history, became also human, redeemed the world and saved the sinful brokenness of earth. In the Lord's progression from Bethlehem to Calvary and beyond to resurrection, God bridged the gap between people and creator. The Lord most definitely chose to "dwell on earth." Not only as a baby, and as a grown man, but after Jesus' death and resurrection, Jesus' spirit willingly takes up residence in each individual life committed to him.

Solomon contemplated the majesty and wondrous divinity of the almighty. How "heaven and the highest heaven cannot contain" him. The traveler approaching her hometown saw its modern buildings rise against the skyline and tried to image that great temple built by Solomon. She imagined herself standing in its courtyard with the sounds of the marketplace all around her. Animals bought and sold, business deals clinched, gossip bartered. In her mind she walked forward into that majestic building and found it to be a place of overpowering stench and awe. The altar covered in the blood of animal sacrifice. The rich trappings of the ark cheek by jowl with dripping knives and drenched measuring scales. Weights and measures and receptacles to cart away the dead carcasses were all foreign to her sensibilities. The atmosphere was as far from her modern Western experience of liturgy as she was prepared to stomach. Yet the procession of the people coming and going was one of deep worship and with a commitment in their eyes which she longed to see in her hometown, and the singing was wonderful.

Long processions of deep-throated incantations that burst the melody through her very toes. Every instrument under the sun, cymbals and trumpets, harps, lutes, timbrels, strings, pipes, they were full of light and joy and such reverence in the dance as made you long to catch the merest glimpse of the object of their worship. God was in the temple and the people showed it.

She thought of how she was to carry God's spirit within her into the modern buildings ahead and knew it would have to be total surrender. To worship with her lifestyle and praise in the shopping malls, banks and streets of home would take some doing. But God never does anything by half measures and she must learn to do the same. To dwell on earth the Lord held nothing back. Costly incarnation requires total response.

Savior, come, take your place
in this poor habitation I call my being,
that all who watch and long to see hope dawn in darkness
will see you dance in me. Amen.

Week 6: Monday
SONG OF JOY
Luke 1:46–55

> *And Mary said,*
>
> *"My soul magnifies the Lord,*
>   *and my spirit rejoices in God my Savior,*
>   *for he has looked with favor on the lowliness of his servant.*
> *Surely, from now on all generations will call me blessed;*
>   *for the Mighty One has done great things for me,*
>   *and holy is his name.*
> *His mercy is for those who fear him*
>   *from generation to generation.*
> *He has shown strength with his arm;*
>   *he has scattered the proud in the thoughts of their hearts.*
> *He has brought down the powerful from their thrones,*
>   *and lifted up the lowly;*
> *he has filled the hungry with good things,*
>   *and sent the rich away empty.*
> *He has helped his servant Israel,*
>   *in remembrance of his mercy,*
>   *according to the promise he made to our ancestors,*
> *to Abraham and to his descendants forever."*

How she must have danced, the traveler thought. How the mother of the baby must have danced when her cousin Elizabeth affirmed the new life within both their wombs. Her song rings down the ages with the freshness and authority of a long-awaited covenant promise. All those sacrifices from ancient days, all the struggles to obey and serve God. All the treks across wilderness after wilderness for Abraham, Isaac, Joseph, come to fruition. Mary's praise of joy expresses the culmination of them all, a new beginning for humankind, and for herself, a new song to sing.

No more waiting, the Christ was on his way, and with the Christ would come the fulfillment of those ancient promises to Israel. A Messiah, a Savior whose coming turns things upside down (which, according to God's wisdom, is really the right way up). The Christ would bring satisfaction for the poor, authority for those without status. Pride, riches, all go to the wall, as a new set of godly priorities takes precedence over previously held sinful and destructive values.

No wonder Mary sang this wonderful song. But for it all to come about, the young girl had to say, "Yes." She had to trust the heavenly vision and agree to the angel Gabriel's message. The Bible recounts how he did not depart from her until after she had agreed that it would be as God had said. We might imagine the angel bursting through the gates of heaven shouting for joy, "She said 'yes'!"

What might have happened if Mary had refused? God, loving and tender as God is, would not have forced the vision, the Lord never does. Oh, God could have found another way to birth the son and bring about the divine purposes for the world, God always can. But, Mary, what a tragedy, if she had missed out on the cooperation with that divine will.

To learn to sing in our hearts, to feel the joy of the dance of the soul, to embrace the pain that pierces our hearts also, is always our choice. The vision is God's, the choice is ours.

The traveler stayed kneeling a long time, considering again the practical implications of bringing the baby home. The difficult struggle to explain what had happened, to those who had been absent from her experience in the stable. The obstacles of the pressures at home, the duties demanding her time, the daily boredom and frustrations of each day's routine tasks. The baby's eyes still shone bright in her memory but when the memory lost its luster, the channel of prayer got blocked with exhaustion, and her home surroundings screamed rational, software-technological logic through the computer screen and onto her fingertips, what then? When everything else is trapped in the virtual, what becomes of reality? Could she carry on singing that new song?

Would the tune fade, the lyrics get confused, or deafened out by a million other tunes along the way? She would not let that happen. God would provide the strength. She would be faithful. God would do the rest.

It was only a few days into the new year and already the problems of the old one were encroaching. She needed to keep singing regardless of the outer circumstances that surrounded her journey and dogged her path. What better song to sing than Mary's— magnifying God more than contemplating her own situation, letting her spirit rejoice rather than dwelling on the negatives; recognizing where she stood in God's sight and God's affection; acknowledging the gratitude she owed to the Lord. Acknowledging God's holiness; God's mercy; God's strength; God's overall control in every circumstance; God's priority for the underdog, the needy; God's perfect sense of justice; God's faithfulness toward the covenant people. When we do all this it is as if we hear God speak our name and whisper, "Happy New Year."

God, I hear it. I hear your earth-shattering,
wonder-filled music of gentle joy and promise.

*Show me no proof, give me no sign, except for your
own presence in me and with me forever. Amen.*

Week 6: Tuesday
GRACE TO BE HOLY
1 Peter 1:13–19

*Therefore prepare your minds for action; discipline yourselves; set
all your hope on the grace that Jesus Christ will bring you when he
is revealed. Like obedient children, do not be conformed to the
desires that you formerly had in ignorance. Instead, as he who
called you is holy, be holy yourselves in all your conduct; for it is
written, "You shall be holy, for I am holy."*

*If you invoke as Father the one who judges all people impartially according to their deeds, live in reverent fear during the time
of your exile. You know that you were ransomed from the futile
ways inherited from your ancestors, not with perishable things like
silver or gold, but with the precious blood of Christ, like that of a
lamb without defect or blemish.*

Ransomed to be free. Our traveler reached the outskirts of the
town with a heart lightened by the enormity of that realization.
Jogging now, she began to move briskly along familiar roads. She
laughed at herself for ever imagining that she could somehow try
hard to be holy. Of course she couldn't, no one can, a human
being can't make him- or herself holy any more than a fish can
make itself dry. The very air we breathe carries the seeds of a broken world, the sin of all humankind. She knew then that the

pursuit of holiness is only possible because God is holy and God's ambition is to make us more and more into Christ's likeness.

"It's a partnership then, is it, God?" she chatted as she jogged. "I mean, I can't change till you change me but you ask for my permission and you expect my unremitting cooperation, right?" And she continued on her way, swerving the passersby who by now thronged the pavements.

Peter had written about "preparing the mind," she thought. It brought back memories of preparation near the beginning of her Advent journey all those weeks ago. The Israelites had needed a strong girding of the physical needs and desires, not to mention the commandments to be kept (ten of them at least), on their arduous trek to the promised land. For herself also the journey had taken its toll. She'd had her luggage jettisoned, her sensibilities affronted, her worldview shattered, her presuppositions challenged, an ugly blister was forming on her big toe, and there was still something unmentionable sticking to the sole of her shoe. But her expectations, ah, now, those had been met far and beyond anything she ever thought was possible.

She wondered about this "preparing the mind" thing. Might a "mind jog" prove more strenuous than a workout at the leisure center? Minds tend to wander a lot, especially with all the TV soaps around. On a good day minds can even be tempted to feel superior, especially with modern media image-makers pushing people into the dangerous occupation of comparing themselves with everybody else.

A good sober "preparing" would do her no harm, she concluded, and what's this about "grace"? It was a word she found hard to define. The nearest she got to understanding it was to compare it with a sensation. Like the feeling of sinking into a wonderful warm bath and experiencing how it smooths the aches of the day away. You just lower yourself into the water but it is the water which graciously soothes. Or like breath to the lungs. You just breathe—the air does the rest. She wouldn't try cataloging or analyzing grace anymore. She would do a spiritual workout until she could accept grace for what it was, a free gift from God.

Dear Lord, your purity gives me hope on my journey.
Please make me holy even as you are holy,
but I need an awful lot of help on the sharp bends.
I pray for strength to be faithful on the temptation corners,
consistent on the long, slow, boring stretches,
and obedient to all that you are and all you call me to be.
And that ransom you paid when the devil
pulled his hijack attempt?
How can I ever pay that back? I can't.
Thank God for grace. Amen.

Week 6: Wednesday
TRUTH TO BE FREE
John 8:31–36

Then Jesus said to the Jews who had believed in him, "If you con-tinue in my word, you are truly my disciples; and you will know the truth, and the truth will make you free." They answered him, "We are descendants of Abraham and have never been slaves to anyone. What do you mean by saying, 'You will be made free'?"

Jesus answered them, "Very truly, I tell you, everyone who commits sin is a slave to sin. The slave does not have a permanent place in the household; the son has a place there forever. So if the Son makes you free, you will be free indeed."

Our traveler was taking truth home. The incredible truth of God's breaking onto the planet in a new and immediate manner. "Good tidings of great joy" for all people. Some people would misinterpret "freedom" just as that baby himself, when grown, was also misinterpreted. Those with their own agendas would make the words political, and the zealots, the "knife-men" of Jesus' day would attempt to hijack the Lord's teaching as justification for acts of terrorism in the attempt to overthrow the Roman authorities. Others would acclaim Jesus as a Savior on Palm Sunday, but only in the hope that the Lord would fulfill their own preconceived ideas of salvation, freedom from poverty, from hardship, a glorious "Santa Claus" salvation of whatever you want, you get.

She had been to Bethlehem, entered the stable, and encountered the child. There were no delusions as she carried the baby home in her mind's thoughts and heart's intentions. "Freedom" was spiritual freedom, not earth-type election promises, quickly broken or ignored.

Could she take home this real truth to a century satiated by shallow media promises of image and advertisement, to a world of convenience foods and disposable relationships? She was bringing the good news that the cruel vasectomy of wonder of spirit could be reversed; that love was not merely a dead concept of a Victorian era; that hope was already fulfilled and could be realized for each man, each woman, in the day-to-day mundane as much as the hyped-up, racy strivings of a glazed-eye generation. Hope was alive and well and living now, upon earth.

Truth applied to the dawning of each Monday morning and the shrill of an alarm clock, to months of winter-depression syndrome, gray and bleak, to the numbing effects of broken family relationships.

She pictured Jesus sitting with the Pharisees who stood upon their own dignity as descendants of Abraham, their pedigree secure, believing themselves to be free men in every sense of the word and unafraid to protest such to Jesus, forerunners of the children of our present age. Protesting their rights, their privileges, their state benefits, their liberty of "coming of age." Liberty to damage their health, to mold their bodies into whatever state or shape they desire, or the image the posters proclaim or their peers seek to emulate. Their rights by birth, by politics, by achievement, they believe are due to them automatically, merely by existing. Personal freedom to be and to do anything and everything in the personal pursuit of happiness. This today is often called "freedom."

Jesus blew a hole right through the concept. First the Savior gave up every right he had in order to visit earth, including the right of divine power, refusing to save himself on the cross, and while here in the flesh Jesus taught that there is an enslavement that comes from sinning which makes slaves of every one of us much more effectively than any other kind of slavery or injustice recognized on earth.

Jesus was free. Free to live, to love, to suffer and to die. Free to save the world through his sacrifice. Now what was it we were protesting about—ah, yes, "happiness."

Jesus, free indeed! I want to be free indeed.
Just like slaves in Bible times, released
when someone bought their freedom,

I thank you, Lord, for paying for my freedom,
not with money but with your life.
I embrace new life in you and, as for happiness,
I leave that in your hands, Lord.
I'm sure you will teach me what it is. Amen.

Week 6: Thursday
THE LEARNING TO LOVE
John 15:12–17

This is my commandment, that you love one another as I have loved you. No one has greater love than this, to lay down one's life for one's friends. You are my friends if you do what I command you. I do not call you servants any longer, because the servant does not know what the master is doing; but I have called you friends, because I have made known to you everything that I have heard from my Father. You did not choose me but I chose you. And I appointed you to go and bear fruit, fruit that will last, so that the Father will give you whatever you ask him in my name. I am giving you these commandments so that you may love one another.

She could hardly believe the truth of it. The son of the living God was declaring personal friendship, with herself. It scared her though, for the Lord's declaration read, ". . . If you do what I command you," and Jesus' greatest command of all was to love.

She had managed to keep the ten commandments pretty well throughout her whole life, even before the journey to Bethlehem. As far as she could remember, no intentional hurt had ever been directed by herself toward even an animal, never mind another human being.

But here was Jesus demanding of the disciples the ultimate sacrifice—love itself. But love was dangerous. It required persons to seek the best welfare of others before their own. It required forgiveness to be extended to the perpetrator, how many times? Not seven, Jesus had said, but seventy-seven, that unit of seven, considered to be a perfect number in the culture of Jesus' day, increased to infinity. In other words, forgiveness, forever and without end.

She thought of a mother's love for her child and what that mother would not do to protect her infant. Of a daughter's love for a righteous father, a son's love for a dedicated and compassionate mother. Limited and incomplete though this earthly love in families is, she nevertheless remembered with awe the beauty and caring of genuine family affection. How could this sacrificial, nonjudgmental, vulnerable love be extended to one another as the Lord commanded?

She wanted to turn on her heels and run back to the stable, to throw herself before the manger and add her sobs of inadequacy to the infant's cries for food.

But she did not need to go back. The risen Christ stood alongside her in her feelings of confusion and fear. Without seeing or hearing Jesus she knew Jesus dwelt within her life. The Savior's words echoed in her mind from the Bible, "You did not choose me, I chose you." If God was doing the choosing, she thought, God would do the loving also. Her part was to relinquish a little more of what had still not been surrendered. Space must be made, a space in her being where love could grow and dwell.

*Lord, I relinquish all negative feelings
to make room for the indwelling of love.
I empty my heart of bitterness
and hatred to make room for your love.
I cancel the tenancy of all old grudges
in order to move love into residence.
I transport all wounds and hurts to the foot of the cross
and allow my tears to mingle with the cries of a dying Savior
that I may share in the Savior's sufferings
which alone could make love possible.*

*I reach out and touch your offer of salvation,
your hand of friendship,
your cleansing power of lordship
that unconditional love may be my healing.*

*I repent of all loveless actions, all unlovely thoughts,
all disobedient living,
that love may not merely be a feeling in me
but an act of my will when the feeling is absent.
A discernment of my spirit when I'm tempted to hate,
a path for the walking of my feet when "un-love"
threatens to deflect my intentions.
Please, God, I come in discipleship to your teaching.
I come for the learning of love.
Vulnerable it will make me as it gives me courage.
A world's victim, I become a friend of the most high.*

*Lord, I recognize now, the real failure
for a follower of yours is the failure to love.
In your name and by your grace teach me,
not merely to show love, but to be love for others. Amen.*

Week 6: Friday
IN HIS LIKENESS
2 Corinthians 3:12–18

Since, then, we have such a hope, we act with great boldness, not like Moses, who put a veil over his face to keep the people of Israel from gazing at the end of the glory that was being set aside. But their minds were hardened. Indeed, to this very day, when they hear the reading of the old covenant, that same veil is still there, since only in Christ is it set aside. Indeed, to this very day whenever Moses is read, a veil lies over their minds; but when one turns to the Lord, the veil is removed. Now the Lord is the Spirit, and where the Spirit of the Lord is, there is freedom. And all of us, with unveiled faces, seeing the glory of the Lord as though reflected in a mirror, are being transformed into the same image from one degree of glory to another; for this comes from the Lord, the Spirit.

Passing through the familiar streets, our traveler contemplated that challenge to "be" love for others. She feared that, like the ancient nomads of Israel, she would find herself in an unending trek across the desert, struggling to keep holy and righteous laws given from God to Moses. The people then were God's chosen ones, chosen to be a witness and a testimony to the surrounding cultures who did not know of Yahweh the one true God.

In Old Testament times God's splendor lay hidden below the veil of Moses. The one true God could not be gazed upon with humankind's naked and sinful eye. The coming of the baby showed earth "God in flesh appearing." As Jesus hung on that cross, the last veiling between God and men and women was removed. It was torn from top to bottom, from God to earth; Jesus' death smashed the final barrier to debts unpaid between a loving God and God's sinful but still-loved children.

Loved but sinful. How could she become "love" for others while still tied to her own imperfections and the imperfection of a broken earth? It would require a new mind, a new heart and a new birth.

Slowly she closed her eyes to all thoughts of the pressures and temptations and frustrations which lay awaiting her amidst the comfortable, provincial spires and shopping malls of home. Whatever lay in wait to ambush her newfound determination to follow the Messiah, she wasn't going to focus upon it just now. For this moment she knew only one thing—she was willing to be remade in the Lord's likeness. For only in the Lord's likeness would love be possible. She must be love with single-minded passion.

Suddenly her eyes shot open in distress. Her mind-pictures were playing footage of visual images from the life of Jesus that put much fear in her heart. Lovely pictures she had known all her life but now she saw what they required in terms of cost.

Jesus was moving among the crowds, touching lepers, grappling with all kinds of diseases, turning no one away, not even when exhausted or when in helping them Jesus' reputation was threatened and his enemies gained ammunition to use against him. Did she want to be made in this likeness?

She thought of Jesus desperate for a rest after constant, demanding toil. Dozing in the bottom of a boat, to be awakened by the wild panic of the disciples as they insisted on "service upon demand" to bring the storm to an end and provide their guarantee of safety. Could she surrender herself to be remade in this likeness? Jesus in Gethsemane facing the anticipation of a violent, brutal death, to say nothing of the emotional agony of betrayal and denial from those the Savior trusted. Suffering the unimaginable pain of the weight of the world's crimes, ills and sins on his own single pair of shoulders and still Jesus forgave. The Savior's likeness, how could she?

Then she saw again that stable, the manger and, in the dim light, the face of the child. The baby's gentle laugh touched her tormented thoughts like the brush of the finger of God and helped her to pray.

Dear Lord, we pray, but it is only by your spirit's power
that we can be remade in your likeness.
You do it; we cannot even make a start.
But you are light, not darkness,
and in that knowledge all things are possible.
For in the remaking is the peace.
In the rebirthing is the life.
Only help us keep our eyes on you.
Not on the fears, or the limitations, only on your face.
The more we see of you,
the less we will fear to take on
your likeness and lose our own. Amen.

Week 6: Saturday
BY HIS STRENGTH
Philippians 3:12–16; 4:12–13

Not that I have already obtained this or have already reached the goal; but I press on to make it my own, because Christ Jesus has made me his own. Beloved, I do not consider that I have made it my own; but this one thing I do: forgetting what lies behind and straining forward to what lies ahead, I press on toward the goal for the prize of the heavenly call of God in Christ Jesus. Let those of us then who are mature be of the same mind; and if you think differently about anything, this too God will reveal to you. Only let us hold fast to what we have attained. . . .

. . . I know what it is to have little, and I know what it is to have plenty. In any and all circumstances I have learned the secret of being well-fed and of going hungry, of having plenty and of being in need. I can do all things through him who strengthens me.

They say the last mile is the longest and so it was for the traveler as she pushed the final button on the last pedestrian crossing before her home. Just one more stretch of road to walk, a few more corners to turn, and she'd be home. Familiar things would surround her once again. She fantasized about the wonderful hot bath she would soak in and thought of the luxury of stretching herself out on the favorite sofa. Faces also came before her mind, her loved ones, friends and colleagues. Pictures of kings, shepherds, fellow travelers, paraded through her memory, each holding out the lessons she had learned, and she knew each had shared with her a gift beyond measure, for through them she had been led to the manger and to the cross, encountered the Savior, and been challenged by what the Savior had done for the love of each human being. She had made a decision and there was no turning back. Her response to Jesus had been a resounding "Yes." Yes to repentance, yes to surrender, yes to change into Jesus' likeness. Spiritually she was bringing the baby home that all those who knew her would, by Jesus' grace, see something of Jesus in her life.

Her arms felt full of him, her heart was filled by him, her joy was real. Within sight of her driveway, she halted. Something was lying on the welcome mat outside her door. It was large and slumped like a backpack. She walked on toward it, puzzled. With her hand on the gate she could see it clearly now. It was her luggage, bulging and bulky, just as she had carried it on the outward journey. Incredulous, she stared at the offending lump. Tears of disappointment came into her eyes and she thought, But I traveled home with such lightness in my step and my heart. I left that all behind, I don't want to be burdened with it again. The thought of unpacking it filled her with dread. I don't need this, she thought, I'm free. God's spirit stilled her fears. "I am your master," God said, "not anything else. These things have no power to hurt or degrade, or hinder. Take control in Jesus' name."

Suddenly she was no longer a slave to the past nor a fugitive escaping the future. She grasped that luggage and flung it with all her strength to the back of the garage. God would deal with it in God's time, in God's way. Daily she would extract piece by piece and, in Christ's strength, allow Christ to remold and recycle it into a tool of Christ's choosing.

Nothing would be wasted, all would be changed. Her life was no longer defined by what she owned or what she had achieved or by her relationships on earth but by that one all-consuming relationship which she had known to be the reason for her journey to the manger. Whatever her situation, good, bad or indifferent, she was living by a strength not her own. These were indeed "good tidings of great joy."

> *Dear Lord, bring me home with joy.*
> *Joy amidst the hard, drab pain of mundane living.*
> *Joy amongst the threatening violence of betrayals from the loved.*
> *Joy amidst the continuing winter of a broken earth.*
> *Soon your clear nights of springtime will return again*
> *but long before they do,*
> *your strength will bring light to the darkest night.*
> *Wasting nothing, I know you can forge gold*
> *from my every moment of dross.*
> *I can wait for your springtime because*
> *"I can do all things in Christ who strengthens me." Amen.*

Moses — the
Egyptians —
fear of the Hebrews
as they populated Egypt — as slaves

Herod — King of